Word to the WISE

A Daily Devotional

Dr. Bill Blocker
President, College of Biblical Studies-Houston

A publication of the College of Biblical Studies

www.cbshouston.edu

Copyright © 2016 William "Bill" Blocker

ISBN: 978-0-9979150-0-6

Cover and text design: Joshua P. Thomas

Word to the Wise audio episodes
Copyright © 2016 William "Bill" Blocker and College of Biblical Studies

Audio engineered, mixed, and mastered by: Joshua P. Thomas

This book is dedicated to my wife, Zelda.

Her unwavering support, patience, and constant inspiration helped me to get Word to the Wise off the ground, on the air, and in this book.

Acknowledgements

If there is one thing that I've learned over the years, it is that success is a team effort. The end product is often the result of a hard working, talented, and passionate team behind the scenes. At the College, I am honored and blessed to have such a team working with me. Three of these team members have taken on the task of transforming our *Word to the Wise* radio devotionals into this written work.

Rick, Melinda, and Josh – Thank you for having my back. I'm proud to serve in the trenches with you!

Rick Kress
Rick oversees theological research and writing, and has taken on the role of production manager for this book.

Melinda Merillat
Melinda is the creative director behind our radio broadcasts, videos, and PR campaigns and has lent her writing, editing, brand expertise, and her ever-watchful PR "eye" to this book.

Joshua Thomas
As our multimedia and graphic design expert, Josh lends incredible talent to all you see and hear regarding the College.

Others of Note
I would be remiss to leave out several others who have given of their time and talents for *Word to the Wise*. To the following, thank you. Your contributions did not go unnoticed:

Lee Bouldin	Dr. Joe Parle
Alicia Collins	Vicki Patterson
Debbie Harper	Dr. Paul Shockley
Sigmund Kramer	The Blocker Children
Bruce Munsterman	

Preface

These brief devotionals were originally recorded for a radio audience. Over time, some of our listeners have expressed a desire to have them in written form. And, this book is the result. At the bottom of each page you will see a QR code. If you would like to hear the audio, scan this code.

The written form and audio files are offered as short words of encouragement and exhortation — obviously not as exhaustive theological studies. Each episode has a biblical principle embedded in it. I have used a wide variety of Bible translations and paraphrases (NASB; NLT; NIV; ESV; NET; HCSB; The Message; my own paraphrase). If you find a quote that begins with "someone said" — someone else said it. You can easily find the source by doing a simple Internet search. I did not want to clutter the reading with citations.

My prayer is that you might find nuggets of truth that help you remember the gospel of grace, and compel you to press on toward the goal of living as a citizen of heaven, though still sojourning on this earth.

As for any wisdom you may see on these pages, it is only because "in Christ are hidden all the treasures of wisdom and knowledge" (Colossians 2:3).

The Best Is yet to Come

Ecclesiastes 7:10

Do you ever think about the good old days?

There is nothing wrong with remembering God's past blessings, but Solomon warns us in Ecclesiastes 7:10, "Do not say why is it that the former days were better than these, for it is not from wisdom that you ask about this."

If you have ever been tempted to long for those good old days, here is a word to the wise.

If you are growing in the grace and knowledge of Christ, you should be wiser today than you were in the good old days. Learn to thank God for yesterday and trust Him for today. Then you will see that **the best is yet to come!**

Today I will apply this wisdom in my life in the following ways:

_____

_____

To listen to this
Word to the Wise,
use your smart device
to scan the QR code!

Calling All Heroes!

Proverbs 16:32

When you think of a hero, what comes to mind?

One preacher said, "There has been more heroism displayed in the household and in the prayer closet than on the most memorable battlefields in history."

If you've only thought of heroes in terms of war or sporting events, here is a word to the wise.

Proverbs 16:32 says, "He who is slow to anger is better than the mighty, and he who rules his spirit than he who captures a city." In God's estimation, patience is more heroic than displays of physical power, and self-control more strategic than capturing a city. Our country, our churches, and our families are in need of more heroes for Christ. Are you one?

Today I will apply this wisdom in my life in the following ways:

_____

_____

To listen to this
Word to the Wise,
use your smart device
to scan the QR code!

January 3

Obviously Obscure

I Thessalonians 5:18

In this world full of challenges and concerns, have you ever wondered what God's will is for you?

Wouldn't it be easier to know exactly how God wants you to approach the big and small issues of life? The Lord has told us exactly what His will is for us. First Thessalonians 5:18 says, "In everything give thanks, for this is God's will for you in Christ Jesus."

If you've missed the obvious while looking for answers to the obscure, here is a word to the wise.

Spend your time seeking to obey God's will and what He *has* revealed, and you won't have time to worry about the things He has chosen *not* to reveal.

Today I will apply this wisdom in my life in the following ways:

_____

_____

To listen to this *Word to the Wise,* use your smart device to scan the QR code!

3

Word to the Wise

Put Your Faith to Work

Hebrews 11:6

When my children were young, I can remember how difficult it was to take my daughter to the doctor for a shot.

As I proceeded to allow the doctor to poke a painful needle into her body, the pain that she encountered caused her to question whether I intended good for her. Sound familiar? Sometimes in life we feel that way about God. Well, according to Hebrews 11:6, it says, "For he who comes to God must believe that He is and that He is a rewarder of those who seek Him."

Are you doubting God's faithfulness? Here is a word to the wise.

When it looks like God doesn't care, put your faith to work, because He is working it out for **your good**!

Today I will apply this wisdom in my life in the following ways:

_____

_____

To listen to this
Word to the Wise,
use your smart device
to scan the QR code!

January 5

Dirty Feet and Divine Blessing

John 13:17

Many of us know that Jesus washed the disciples' feet the night He was betrayed.

Many of us know that He calls believers to humbly serve one another in love. Jesus said, in John 13:17, "If you know these things, you are blessed if you do them." Do you know these things?

Here is a word to the wise.

Simply *knowing* the truth of Jesus' love and His commandment to love one another does not bring divine blessing. Only those who humble themselves and actively serve others know God's blessings. So, what are you waiting for? Find some dirty, stinky feet and start washing!

Today I will apply this wisdom in my life in the following ways:

_____

_____

To listen to this
Word to the Wise,
use your smart device
to scan the QR code!

January 6

An Offer You Can't Refuse

Joel 2:13

Some Christians believe that sin goes away with time.

Here's a newsflash — while you may desire to brush it off, time does not do away with sin.

God encourages us in Joel 2, "Yet even now return to the Lord your God for He is gracious and compassionate, slow to anger, abounding in lovingkindness, and relenting of evil."

If you're waiting for your sin to go away in time, here is a word to the wise.

Don't waste any more time. God is offering you, even now, the opportunity to return in wholehearted repentance.

Today I will apply this wisdom in my life in the following ways:

_____

_____

To listen to this
Word to the Wise,
use your smart device
to scan the QR code!

January 7

Don't Settle for Close Enough

Genesis 17:15-19

Sometimes we can confuse contentment with complacency.

In Genesis 17, God promised a nearly 100-year-old Abraham a son through Sarah, who was 90. Abraham laughed at what seemed to be impossible and essentially told God that Ishmael, his son by Hagar, would work as the promised heir. But God did not see Abraham's solution as an option.

If you've adjusted your understanding of God's promises to fit your current circumstances, here is a word to the wise.

Your relationship with God is not like the game of Horseshoes. Trust His Word and be patient. Don't settle for "close enough."

Today I will apply this wisdom in my life in the following ways:

_____

_____

To listen to this
Word to the Wise,
use your smart device
to scan the QR code!

January 8

Source of Troubles

Psalm 51:4

John Maxwell said, "If you could kick the person most responsible for most of your troubles, you wouldn't be able to sit down for weeks."

Although David was a man after God's heart, he had his share of self-inflicted problems. He could have blamed the stresses from running the kingdom for his mistakes; however, in Psalm 51:4, he says, "Against You, You only, I have sinned and done wrong what is evil in Your sight."

Are you blaming others for your problems? Here is a word to the wise.

Your problems will never be resolved until you acknowledge that you are the source. Stop blaming others for your failure. Repent and God will allow you to sit comfortably in His presence.

Today I will apply this wisdom in my life in the following ways:

_____

_____

To listen to this
Word to the Wise,
use your smart device
to scan the QR code!

January 9

Spice It Up!

Colossians 3:12

A sixth-century Chinese philosopher once said, "Marriage is three parts love and seven parts forgiveness of sin."

Does your marriage have the right mix? Paul says in Colossians 3:12, "So, as those who have been chosen of God, holy and beloved, put on a heart of compassion, kindness, humility, gentleness, and patience, bearing with one another and forgiving each other."

If you want to improve your marriage, here is a word to the wise.

While you're waiting on your spouse to do their part by adding compassion, kindness, and humility; add gentleness, patience, and forgiveness to *your* recipe. It will surely spice up your marriage.

Today I will apply this wisdom in my life in the following ways:

_____

_____

To listen to this
Word to the Wise,
use your smart device
to scan the QR code!

January 10

Praising God Through the Tough Stuff

Philippians 4:4

Oftentimes, sports players will praise God after scoring a touchdown, hitting a homerun, or even winning a game, but how many have you seen praise Him after fumbling the football, striking out, or losing the game?

This sounds similar to our faith walk. We have no problem praising God after something amazing happens in our life, but how frequently do we praise Him during the tough stuff?

The Bible commands us to rejoice always. Philippians 4:4 says, "Rejoice in the Lord always. Again, I say, rejoice."

Here is a word to the wise.

Ask God to help you, like Paul, praise God in the midst of your trials and **experience true rejoicing**!

Today I will apply this wisdom in my life in the following ways:

_____

_____

To listen to this
Word to the Wise,
use your smart device
to scan the QR code!

January 11

Walk by Faith, Not by Feelings

John 12:27

Have you ever felt overwhelmed by circumstances you were facing?

Just prior to the ordeal of the cross, Jesus said in John 12:27, "Now My soul has become troubled, and what should I say? Father, save Me from this hour? For this purpose I came to this hour. Father, glorify Your name." He knew that the Father wanted Him to face and embrace the cross.

If you want a way out of your trial, here is a word to the wise.

Conquer your emotions by obeying God's Word no matter how you feel. Walk by faith, not by feelings, and God will glorify His name through you – even in your trial.

Today I will apply this wisdom in my life in the following ways:

_____

_____

To listen to this
Word to the Wise,
use your smart device
to scan the QR code!

January 12

Release the Right to Avenge the Wrong

Luke 23:34

Has someone hurt you and they want your forgiveness, but they really haven't repented for the wrong they've done?

Do you wonder sometimes how Jesus would have handled these situations? In Luke 23:34, while on the cross, Jesus says, "Father, forgive them for they do not know what they are doing." I'm still amazed that Jesus could look at them as they were hurling insults and ask God to forgive them.

By asking for their forgiveness, Jesus was releasing the right to avenge the wrong. Here is a word to the wise.

God asks us to release the right to avenge the wrong for those who hurt us. If the sinless Savior could do the same for us, He expects nothing less from you.

Today I will apply this wisdom in my life in the following ways:

_____

_____

To listen to this
Word to the Wise,
use your smart device
to scan the QR code!

January 13

Pathway to Peace

I Peter 5:6-7

Do you ever feel anxious and depressed by the cares of this life?

All of us, including Jesus and the apostle Paul, have felt the burdens of life in a fallen world. But letting these cares become a reason to constantly worry or to become depressed is *not* the answer.

If you're wondering if there's a real answer, here is a word to the wise.

First Peter 5:6-7 says, "Therefore, humble yourselves under the mighty hand of God, casting all your anxiety on Him, because He cares for you." Stop looking to yourself for answers. Trust the Lord. Pride is at the root of anxiety. Humility is the pathway to peace.

Today I will apply this wisdom in my life in the following ways:

_____

_____

To listen to this
Word to the Wise,
use your smart device
to scan the QR code!

January 14

Seeing Is Not Necessarily Believing

Hebrews 11:1

We've all heard the statement, "Seeing is believing."

The Bible says that faith is believing even in what we cannot see. Philip Yancey once said, "Faith is believing in advance what makes sense in reverse."

It is easy to look back over our lives and see God's hand of providence, but it's much harder to look forward with the same eyes of certainty than we can looking back. Hebrews 11:1 says, "Now faith is the assurance of things hoped for, the conviction of things not seen."

Do you need to see before you believe? Here is a word to the wise.

If your faith is only in what you see, ask God to increase your faith in what you can't see – Him!

Today I will apply this wisdom in my life in the following ways:

_____

_____

To listen to this
Word to the Wise,
use your smart device
to scan the QR code!

14

January 15

Behold the Lamb of Glory!

John 1:29; Isaiah 53

Do you remember the statement from John the Baptist about Jesus when he said, "Behold the Lamb of God who takes away the sin of the world!"

Did you know that John said this after Jesus' wilderness temptation? The Lamb of God was likely skin and bones after His 40-day fast.

If you've never considered the setting of John's declaration, here is a word to the wise.

Isaiah 53 prophesied that the Messiah would have no stately form or majesty nor appearance that we should be attracted to Him, but He would offer Himself a guilt offering for sinners. Jesus is still unimpressive to most, but those of us who know our need, **praise Him as the Lamb of Glory**.

Today I will apply this wisdom in my life in the following ways:

_____

_____

To listen to this
Word to the Wise,
use your smart device
to scan the QR code!

January 16

It's All in the Attitude

Matthew 6:14

The Rev. Martin Luther King, Jr., has said, "Forgiveness is not an occasional act. It is a permanent attitude."

In Matthew 6, Jesus says, "If you don't forgive men, then your Father will not forgive your transgressions."

Are you holding grudges? Here is a word to the wise.

It's all about attitude. A lack of forgiveness reveals a major blind spot in our spiritual vision. If our sin against an infinitely holy God can be forgiven, we must forgive others who sin against us. The next time you say, "I'm never gonna forgive!" <u>remember what Christ did for you</u>. Now, that's an attitude of gratitude!

Today I will apply this wisdom in my life in the following ways:

_____

_____

To listen to this
Word to the Wise,
use your smart device
to scan the QR code!

January 17

No Compromise

Jeremiah 37

In a world that pressures Christians to keep quiet about our faith, how do you live a life without compromise?

Let's take a lesson from Jeremiah. In Chapter 37, God told him to deliver a disturbing message to Zedekiah, the puppet king of Judah. He told the king that the Chaldeans would return, capture, and burn down the city of Judah, a truth that would cause him to be thrown in prison and beaten. Why? Because he did not compromise.

Here is a word to the wise.

God is faithful. He will not let you be tempted beyond what you can bear. Stand firm in your faith and don't waver!

Today I will apply this wisdom in my life in the following ways:

_____

_____

To listen to this
Word to the Wise,
use your smart device
to scan the QR code!

January 18

Father Knows Best

Psalm 65:5

My granddaughter has reached the inquisitive age in life, the age around two to four where most communication comes in the form of a question.

"Papa, why is God invisible?" The response to any answer given is always the same, "But, Papa, why?" Sometimes as Christians, we, rather than trust His promises, are like my granddaughter asking why. "Why me?"

If your circumstances are leading you to question God, here is a word to the wise.

Psalm 65:5 says, "By awesome deeds, you answer us with deliverance." Only in God's Word will you find rest. Through faith you will discover that **He** knows what's best.

Today I will apply this wisdom in my life in the following ways:

_____

_____

To listen to this
Word to the Wise,
use your smart device
to scan the QR code!

January 19

The Biblical Environmentalist

Isaiah 24:5

In this day and age, many people are very worried about the environment.

We receive many requests to do things to preserve our future; however, there's a greater threat to our environment than pollutants.

Isaiah 24:5 says, "The earth is also polluted by its inhabitants."

If you are really concerned about the earth, here is a word to the wise.

Sin literally pollutes the earth. It stirs up evil, hatred, and it starts wars and every form of destruction. Pray that God would turn the hearts of people back to Him so that **His will** would be done on earth.

Today I will apply this wisdom in my life in the following ways:

_____

_____

To listen to this
Word to the Wise,
use your smart device
to scan the QR code!

January 20

Every Tear

Psalm 56:8

How many tears have you shed so far in your lifetime?

Amazingly, God counts your every tear. He knows and cares about the sorrows of His own.

In Psalm 56:8, it says, "You keep track of all my sorrows. You have collected all my tears in your bottle. You have recorded each one in Your book."

When you are afraid and sorrowful, where do you turn for hope? Here is a word to the wise.

Yes, you will face times of tears in this fallen world. As David says, "When I am afraid, I will put my trust in You." Trust God. He counts your tears and *He cares for you.*

Today I will apply this wisdom in my life in the following ways:

_____

_____

To listen to this
Word to the Wise,
use your smart device
to scan the QR code!

January 21

In the Fire
Daniel 3:17

Dr. Martin Luther King, Jr. said, "There comes a time when one must take a position that is neither safe nor political nor popular, but he must take it because his conscience tells him it is right."

As we look at the ongoing crises in our nation, it is time to take a biblical stand.

If your conscience is screaming at you to stand up but your fears are telling you to sit down, here is a word to the wise.

Heed the actions of the three Hebrew boys in Daniel Chapter 3. They believed that God had the power to deliver them but were willing to suffer the consequences if He did not. Sometimes the solution for our crisis is found *in the fire*, where God is right there with us.

Today I will apply this wisdom in my life in the following ways:

_____

_____

To listen to this *Word to the Wise*, use your smart device to scan the QR code!

Eyes of Faith

Ecclesiastes 8:12

Have you ever struggled with the reality that sometimes wicked people prosper and those who love God do not?

Solomon saw the same problem, but he calls us to hold on in faith. In Ecclesiastes 8:12, he wrote, "Although a sinner does evil a hundred times and may lengthen his life, still I know that it will be well for those who fear God, who fear Him openly."

If you're having trouble making sense of the injustice of it all, here is a word to the wise.

God is just. He *will* deal with the wicked and He *will* openly honor those who openly fear Him. With eyes of faith, look beyond this world to the reality of eternity.

Today I will apply this wisdom in my life in the following ways:

_____

_____

To listen to this
Word to the Wise,
use your smart device
to scan the QR code!

January 23

I Can Do *Without* All Things

Philippians 4:13

It has been said, "The more we count the blessings we have, the less we crave the luxuries we don't have."

Paul wrote in Philippians 4, "I've learned the secret of living in every situation, whether it is with a full stomach or empty, with plenty or little."

If you really want to know the secret to contentment, here is a word to the wise.

Paul says, "I can do everything through Christ who gives me strength." Jesus doesn't always give us earthly riches. So stop complaining about the things you don't have, and count your many blessings for the things you do have in Christ."

Today I will apply this wisdom in my life in the following ways:

_____

_____

To listen to this
Word to the Wise,
use your smart device
to scan the QR code!

January 24

Shooing Flies with an Ax

Galations 6:1

Someone said, "Do not remove a fly from your friend's forehead with a hatchet."

The apostle Paul would agree. In Galatians 6:1, he wrote, "Brethren, even if anyone is caught in a trespass, you who are spiritual restore such a one in the spirit of gentleness."

If you've ever wielded the ax a little too hard, here is a word to the wise.

None of us are fond of flies, but your goal should be to help, not to take someone else's scalp. When addressing someone's sin, put your hatchet away. Use the tools of humility, prayer, and the Word of God. You're more likely to actually kill the fly and avoid being a real <u>headache</u> to your friend!

Today I will apply this wisdom in my life in the following ways:

_____

_____

To listen to this
Word to the Wise,
use your smart device
to scan the QR code!

What's for Dinner?

Proverbs 10:19

As they say, the best time to eat crow is while it's still hot.

Have you ever said anything you wish you could take back? Proverbs 10:19 says, "Where there are many words, transgression is unavoidable, but he who restrains his lips is wise."

If you're having trouble taming your tongue, here is a word to the wise.

Unlike those who feel the need to say everything that comes to mind, take a moment to think before you speak. It just may keep you from sinning – and having to eat roasted crow for dinner.

Today I will apply this wisdom in my life in the following ways:

_____

_____

To listen to this
Word to the Wise,
use your smart device
to scan the QR code!

Never Alone

Psalm 34:18

I once heard a powerful quote that said, "Love comes to those who still hope even though they've been disappointed, to those who still believe even though they've been betrayed, and to those who still love even though they've been hurt before."

Psalm 34:18 says, "The Lord is near to the brokenhearted and saves those who are crushed in spirit."

Do you have a broken heart or a crushed spirit? Here is a word to the wise.

How would you know God is near to the brokenhearted if He never allowed your heart to be broken? God promises to be nearest to us in our lowest moments. So, be assured. If your heart is broken, God is near.

Today I will apply this wisdom in my life in the following ways:

_____

To listen to this
Word to the Wise,
use your smart device
to scan the QR code!

January 27

Too Busy for Prayer?

Acts 6:4

As a president and pastor, my schedule gets pretty busy.

I get numerous demands from multiple people. It's very easy for me to allow those demands to crowd out my time with God.

The apostles found themselves in the same situation after exponential growth in the early church. For this reason they appointed deacons to help them. I found the reason why in Acts 6:4. It's interesting. "We will devote ourselves to prayer and to the ministry of the Word."

If you are a busy body, here is a word to the wise.

Don't let your busy schedule crowd out your quality time with God. If the apostles, who had the difficult task of building the early church, made time for prayer and God's Word, so should we!

Today I will apply this wisdom in my life in the following ways:

_____

_____

To listen to this
Word to the Wise,
use your smart device
to scan the QR code!

January 28

There's Work to Do

II Timothy 2:2

Do you know that we all have a role to play in training the next generation of believers?

In II Timothy 2:2, Paul says, "These things you've heard from me in the presence of many witnesses, entrust to faithful men who will be able to teach others also." Here at the College of Biblical Studies, we are entrusting the truth of the Scriptures to those who are teaching others and we're seeing transformation.

If you haven't given much thought to training the next generation, here is a word to the wise.

Never underestimate your role in prayer, service, and financial support. Why? Because as a believer, your role in ministry is vital.

Today I will apply this wisdom in my life in the following ways:

_____

_____

To listen to this
Word to the Wise,
use your smart device
to scan the QR code!

Bread of Life

John 6

It's been said, "The cost of food in the kingdom is hunger for the Bread of Life."

In John 6, the crowds wanted to make Jesus king after He miraculously fed them. The next day, however, they demanded He continue to feed them. Jesus told them, "I am the Bread of Life that comes down from heaven." In other words, I am much more important than food. I am life itself. The crowds were not happy with Jesus' answer. Most of them left.

How do you respond when Jesus doesn't give you what you ask for? Here is a word to the wise.

God may not always give you what you think you want, but if you hunger for Jesus, you have everything you'll ever need.

Today I will apply this wisdom in my life in the following ways:

_____

_____

To listen to this
Word to the Wise,
use your smart device
to scan the QR code!

January 30

The B.I.B.L.E.

Deuteronomy 8:2

Do you ever feel in life like you're in a perpetual maze?

In reality, some people are so busy going so fast, they don't realize the road they're traveling on leads to nowhere. I call this the wilderness complex, choosing to do things your way at any cost.

How many years have you wasted, wandering in the wilderness? This is what happened to the Israelites for forty years. Why? According to Deuteronomy 8:2, it says that God allowed them to wander so that He may humble them to test their heart and to know whether they would keep His commandments.

If you're in need of new directions in life, here is a word to the wise.

Commit yourself to reading the **b**asic **i**nstructions **b**efore **l**eaving **e**arth – the Bible!

Today I will apply this wisdom in my life in the following ways:

_____

_____

To listen to this
Word to the Wise,
use your smart device
to scan the QR code!

January 31

People Not Like You

Luke 15:2

Jesus spent a lot of time with people that society rejected – the poor, the sinners, the sick.

In fact, Jesus spent so much time with them that the religious leaders of His day said in Luke 15:2, "This man receives sinners and eats with them."

How do you view people who are not like you? Here is a word to the wise.

Oddly, the people that the world casts out are the very people Jesus calls us to love. Even Jesus says in Matthew, "What you do to the least of these you're also doing to Me."

Here's a question for you. How are you doing with the least of these?

Today I will apply this wisdom in my life in the following ways:

_____

_____

To listen to this
Word to the Wise,
use your smart device
to scan the QR code!

February 1

Hidden Treasures

Proverbs 2:1-5

If you knew someone had buried a million dollars in your backyard, how much of your property would you dig up until you found the treasure?

Proverbs 2 indicates, if we seek God's Word as silver and search for it as a hidden treasure, then we will discern the fear of the Lord and discover the knowledge of God. Unfortunately, most of us struggle to find the discipline to dig for the true treasure in God's Word.

If you're spending more time digging for fool's gold than searching the Scriptures, here is a word to the wise.

God promises to reveal Himself to those who diligently seek Him. If you want to find true treasure that never loses its value, seek God and dig into His Word.

Today I will apply this wisdom in my life in the following ways:

_____

_____

To listen to this
Word to the Wise,
use your smart device
to scan the QR code!

32

February 2

Obedience

II Corinthians 5:15

A man once said to me, "Obedience is a strong word when it comes to religion."

I asked him, "If you were dying and someone saved you from death, how would you respond?" He said to me, "I'd probably do anything he wanted." You can probably guess what I said next.

Here's a question for you. As a Christian, are you living out your obedience to God's Word? If not, here is a word to the wise.

Paul says in II Corinthians 5:15, "He died for all so that they who live might no longer live for themselves but for Him who died and rose again on their behalf." May the love of Christ compel you to **live** for Him and to **obey** Him!

Today I will apply this wisdom in my life in the following ways:

_____

_____

To listen to this *Word to the Wise*, use your smart device to scan the QR code!

February 3

Everyday Battles

Joshua 17:13

One writer said, "The Christian faith is not so much proved by his faith in a sudden crisis as by his faithfulness in daily living."

Israel in Joshua's day was able to win great victories against nations more numerous and powerful than they. But in the years following Joshua's leadership, the work of possessing the land over a long period of time became something they chose not to do.

If you find heroism to be more attractive than long-term obedience, here is a word to the wise.

Don't settle for short-lived displays of faith. See every day, every thought, every word as a battle for the glory of God – and the well-being of your soul.

Today I will apply this wisdom in my life in the following ways:

_____

_____

To listen to this
Word to the Wise,
use your smart device
to scan the QR code!

February 4

God's Witness Protection Program

II Corinthians 5:17

We've all heard about the United States witness protection program.

Through this service, these witnesses get a fresh start on life with new identities. Why? About ninety-five percent of them are criminals.

While we may not be criminals ourselves, we do have a sinful past. The good news is that God has a witness protection program that has been working for over two thousand years. According to II Corinthians 5:17, "If anyone is in Christ, he is a new creation. The old has passed away. Behold, all things have become new."

If you're discouraged about your past, here is a word to the wise.

God has given you a new identity in Jesus Christ. Use this identity to live for Christ with no regret!

Today I will apply this wisdom in my life in the following ways:

_____

_____

To listen to this
Word to the Wise,
use your smart device
to scan the QR code!

February 5

Storm Alert

Genesis 7:23

Charles Spurgeon said, "It is shocking to reflect that the change in the weather has more effect on some men's lives than the dread alternative of heaven or hell."

Sadly, in Noah's day, a change in the weather ended in a multitude facing divine judgment. Genesis 7:23 records, "God blotted out every living thing, and only Noah and his family were left in the ark."

If the weather forecast seems more relevant for today than some distant day of reckoning, here is a word to the wise.

There is coming a storm of God's judgment on sin. Enter the ark of salvation through Jesus Christ and live.

Today I will apply this wisdom in my life in the following ways:

_____

_____

To listen to this
Word to the Wise,
use your smart device
to scan the QR code!

February 6

Can You Hear Me Now?

Exodus 2:23

When we are in pain, the enemy whispers in our ear that God does not care for us.

Did you know that the very nature of God is to be deeply concerned for those who suffer? In Exodus 2:23 the sons of Israel groaned because of the bondage. They cried out and their cry for help rose up to God.

If you are beginning to doubt God's care for you, here is a word to the wise.

God does not ignore the cries of His children. The same God who used Moses to deliver His people out of captivity is the one to whom you can turn to in the midst of your suffering. Stop listening to those voices! God sees your sufferings and hears your cries!

Today I will apply this wisdom in my life in the following ways:

_____

_____

To listen to this
Word to the Wise,
use your smart device
to scan the QR code!

Word to the Wise

Confidence in God

Psalm 56:3-4

It has been said, "The time of fear is the time to trust."

No doubt, God calls us to trust Him in every circumstance we face, whether we feel fulfilled or fearful. But Psalm 56:3-4 does indeed confirm that the time of fear is the time to trust. It says, "When I am afraid, I will put my trust in You, in God, whose Word I praise. In God, I have put my trust. I shall not be afraid."

When you are afraid of what you're facing, here is a word to the wise.

If you are a believer, make a choice to put your confidence in God and His Word, and not in your circumstances.

Today I will apply this wisdom in my life in the following ways:

_____

_____

To listen to this
Word to the Wise,
use your smart device
to scan the QR code!

February 8

Pleasing God
Hebrews 11:6

Young children often try to come up with ways to please their parents.

For instance, they draw a picture, hoping that their parents will like it.

What most kids don't realize is that their parents are pleased just to have their love. They don't put the pictures on the refrigerator because they're Rembrandts; they put them on the refrigerator because the artist is the person whom the parents love.

How do we as Christians please God? Here is a word to the wise.

Hebrews 11:6 says, "And without faith it is impossible to please Him." If you desire to please God, simply trust Him today.

Today I will apply this wisdom in my life in the following ways:

_____

_____

To listen to this
Word to the Wise,
use your smart device
to scan the QR code!

February 9

You Can Find It on *Faithbook*

Romans 12:2

A.W. Tozer said, "The things you read will fashion you by slowly conditioning your mind."

What conditions *your* mind? Facebook posts? Twitter feeds? Internet blogs? News feeds? Romans 12:2 reminds us not to be conformed to this world but to be transformed by the renewing of our minds.

If you're not as careful about what you read as you should be, here is a word to the wise.

Sift whatever you read, watch, or even listen to through the Word of God first. Over time, you'll find yourself fashioned more and more into the image of Christ rather than a selfie of the world.

Today I will apply this wisdom in my life in the following ways:

_____

_____

To listen to this
Word to the Wise,
use your smart device
to scan the QR code!

February 10

Weariness to Worship

II Thessalonians 3:13

Do you ever feel tired of doing what is right because it doesn't seem to make a difference?

Evidently, the Thessalonian church knew the same feeling. The apostle Paul wrote in II Thessalonians 3:13, "But as for you, brethren, do not grow weary of doing good."

If you're feeling weary in your walk with Christ, here is a word to the wise.

Don't focus on what others are doing or not doing. Rather, focus on Christ's relentless pursuit of obeying God's will and sacrifice to redeem us from our sin. As you do, your weariness will give way to worship – and your disappointment will give way to determination to live for the One who gave Himself up for *you*.

Today I will apply this wisdom in my life in the following ways:

_____

_____

To listen to this
Word to the Wise,
use your smart device
to scan the QR code!

41

February 11

Who's Got the Power?

Mark 3:16-19

Have you noticed that in the Bible God often selects people whom we would consider to be less than average?

If we were in charge of saving the world, we would probably, according to human standards, recruit the most intelligent people with the highest IQ to complete the assignment.

On the contrary, Jesus selected twelve ordinary men who were not considered brilliant, but they transformed the world.

Here is a word to the wise.

Don't throw in the towel because you don't think you have what it takes. God uses ordinary people to do extraordinary things. Why? To show that the surpassing power belongs to God and not to us!

Today I will apply this wisdom in my life in the following ways:

_____

_____

To listen to this
Word to the Wise,
use your smart device
to scan the QR code!

Follow the Leader

John 10:27-28

Do you remember the children's game, *Follow the Leader?* The leader tries to eliminate those following him by leading them in ways and places they can't or don't want to go.

If you feel like you want to drop out in your walk with Christ, here is a word to the wise.

Jesus said in John 10:27-28, "My sheep hear My voice and I know them and they follow Me, and I give eternal life to them and they will never perish and no one will snatch them out of My hand."

No matter how difficult it may seem for the moment, Christ is not trying to get you out. Keep listening to Jesus! The Good Shepherd guarantees that you will win.

Today I will apply this wisdom in my life in the following ways:

_____

_____

To listen to this *Word to the Wise*, use your smart device to scan the QR code!

Only You Can Prevent Tongue Fires

James 3

Did you know that according to the forest fire statistics, nine out of ten forest fires originate from human cause?

As Christians, are you aware of the fires we can start with our words? Take this test. If my tongue were a type of candy, what would it be — a jawbreaker or cotton candy? James 3 says, "The tongue is a small member, but yet it boasts of great things. How great a forest fire is set ablaze by such a small fire."

Here is a word to the wise.

Woe to those who are often criticizing, gossiping, and joking. Ask God to help you listen to those around you and stop the roasting.

Today I will apply this wisdom in my life in the following ways:

_____

_____

To listen to this
Word to the Wise,
use your smart device
to scan the QR code!

February 14

Love's Like a Hurricane

Romans 8:39

Love's like a hurricane and I am a tree ("How He Loves").

I'm sure you've sung this line before, or at least heard this on the radio, but have you really pondered it?

Jesus loves you. This is quite a cliché to some of us, and we often brush it off without even thinking about the words.

Have you ever felt like you were all alone? Here is a word to the wise.

In Romans 8:39, we are told that nothing can separate us from the love of God. So, no matter what happens in your life, Christ will always be there for you. Remember that love *is* like a hurricane and *you* are the tree — *bending beneath the weight of His glory.*

Today I will apply this wisdom in my life in the following ways:

_____

_____

To listen to this
Word to the Wise,
use your smart device
to scan the QR code!

February 15

Watch Out!

Genesis 20

Have you ever experienced a long period of victory over some particular sin only to see it unexpectedly rear its ugliness a few years later?

In Genesis 20, out of fear, Abraham lied about Sarah not being his wife, something he had done some 25 years earlier. God had to intervene to protect Sarah from being taken as another man's wife. Even godly people can be spiritually weak at times, but praise be to God that His grace and His power are greater than our sin.

If you've ever been surprised by your dormant sin, here is a word to the wise.

Never overestimate your spiritual maturity. Cling to Jesus. He is our only deliverer from sin.

Today I will apply this wisdom in my life in the following ways:

_____

_____

To listen to this
Word to the Wise,
use your smart device
to scan the QR code!

February 16

Messes of Life

John 4

Have you ever messed up so badly that it left you feeling hopeless?

If the answer is yes, then you're in good company, because we all have. In John Chapter 4, Jesus encounters a woman at the well while she performs one of the most mundane tasks in her messed-up life, drawing water out of the well. Jesus performs a miracle through the mundane. He grants her forgiveness.

If you're trying to recover from one of your bad decisions, here is a word to the wise.

Admit that you've messed up to God. In prayer, ask Him to forgive you. While this may not correct your messy past, it will give you bright hope for the future.

Today I will apply this wisdom in my life in the following ways:

_____

_____

To listen to this *Word to the Wise,* use your smart device to scan the QR code!

February 17

God-Reliant

Psalm 30:11

Paul David Tripp said, "Despair is a good thing. Why? Because, if you think that you can dwell on God's holy hill by your own merit, you're going to crush yourself. You need to give up all hope in your own righteousness and rely on Christ."

If your self-reliance is bringing you sorrow, here is a word to the wise.

In Psalm 30:11 it says, "You have turned for me my mourning into dancing. You have loosed my sackcloth and girded me with gladness." God often takes our despair and turns it into gladness, but He wants us to turn our self-reliance into reliance upon Him.

Today I will apply this wisdom in my life in the following ways:

_____

_____

To listen to this
Word to the Wise,
use your smart device
to scan the QR code!

February 18

Is It Time to Get Your Eyes Checked?

John 9:39

Helen Keller said, "The only thing worse than being blind is having sight but no vision."

In John 9, Jesus healed the blind man on the Sabbath and the Pharisees were angry that Jesus didn't conform to their religious traditions. Jesus said, "For judgment I have come into this world so that the blind will see and those who see will become blind."

How can you tell if you are in need of corrective surgery? Here is a word to the wise.

Jesus is the measure of man's spiritual vision. Those who believe He is God and worship Him see clearly. Those who want Him to conform to their expectations are blind. How about you? **Have you had your eye exam lately?**

Today I will apply this wisdom in my life in the following ways:

_____

_____

To listen to this
Word to the Wise,
use your smart device
to scan the QR code!

February 19

Do the Dirty Work

Proverbs 14:4

Shoveling manure is not a pleasant chore, but it may have its advantages.

Proverbs 14:4 says, "Where no oxen are, the manger is clean, but much revenue comes by the strength of the ox." Sometimes we have to do the dirty work before we reap the rewards of a job well done.

If you struggle with seeing the long-term benefits of difficult labor now, here is a word to the wise.

Don't give up because something is difficult or disagreeable. If something is not pleasant for the moment, *don't give up.* Plug your nose and keep on scooping! Your reward is coming.

Today I will apply this wisdom in my life in the following ways:

_____

_____

To listen to this
Word to the Wise,
use your smart device
to scan the QR code!

February 20

Go for the Glory!

Proverbs 19:11

Abraham Lincoln once gave an order to his Secretary of War Edwin Stanton, who promptly declared to the messenger that Lincoln was, let's just say, "a [darned] fool." Upon hearing this response, the President said, "If Stanton said I was 'a [darned] fool', I must be one, for he's nearly always right and generally says what he means."

If your first reaction would have been to fire Stanton, here is a word to the wise.

Proverbs 19:11 says, "A man's discretion makes him slow to anger, and it is his glory to overlook a transgression." The next time someone offends you, go for the glory! **Overlook the offense.**

Today I will apply this wisdom in my life in the following ways:

_____

_____

To listen to this *Word to the Wise,* use your smart device to scan the QR code!

February 21

Rice Christians

Matthew 10:38

A.W. Tozer said, "By playing down the cost of discipleship, we are producing rice Christians."

This is a term used to reference those who adopt Christianity for profit or gain. The experienced missionary knows that the convert must pay a heavy price for his faith in Christ.

If you've been told that being a Christian is an easy street, here is a word to the wise.

Jesus said in Matthew 10:38, "Whoever does not take up his cross and follow Me is not worthy of Me." The denial of self-interest and desires may cost you a lot, but when you make a commitment to do the will of God, **nothing** can compare.

Today I will apply this wisdom in my life in the following ways:

_____

_____

To listen to this
Word to the Wise,
use your smart device
to scan the QR code!

Trusting in Him

Isaiah 55:8

Once, a father saw his little girl, Natalie, about to jump into the deep end of the pool and she did not know how to swim.

He yelled, "Natalie, no!" Natalie stopped in her tracks and cried because her father yelled so loud and prevented her from getting into the pool. Little did she know that her father was saving her life!

Does it seem that God is shouting "NO!" to you? Here is a word to the wise.

Isaiah 55:8 says, "For My thoughts are not your thoughts, nor your ways My ways, declares the Lord." Even if it appears that God is trying to keep you from doing something wonderful, trust Him. He may be keeping you from harm.

Today I will apply this wisdom in my life in the following ways:

_____

_____

To listen to this
Word to the Wise,
use your smart device
to scan the QR code!

February 23

Eternal Guarantee

Genesis 1:1; Isaiah 46:10

"In the beginning, God created the heavens and the earth." Have you ever thought about the eternity of God?

He has always existed eternally with all knowledge, power, and wisdom. There was never a time when God did not know everything there is to know about you.

So why does this matter? Here is a word to the wise.

He said in Isaiah 46:10, "Only I can tell you the future before it happens. Everything I plan will come to pass." God has declared that those who trust in Jesus will overcome death. If you truly believe in Christ, you are eternally secure. The eternal God guarantees it.

Today I will apply this wisdom in my life in the following ways:

_____

_____

To listen to this
Word to the Wise,
use your smart device
to scan the QR code!

February 24

Prescription for Anti-Aging

John 11:25

Recently, the news reported that a new diabetes drug may have antiaging effects to the tune of extending life to 120 years.

Most of us want to enjoy good health and extend our lives, but all of us will one day face the inevitable reality of physical death. Jesus said in John 11:25, "I am the resurrection and the life. He who believes in Me will live even if he dies."

If you're tempted to be more concerned about your health than heavenly realities, here is a word to the wise.

Health is important, but it can't compare to eternal life. If you want to truly live now and forever, Jesus is the only answer.

Today I will apply this wisdom in my life in the following ways:

_____

_____

To listen to this
Word to the Wise,
use your smart device
to scan the QR code!

February 25

Highway Humility Instead of Road Rage

Philippians 2:3

As you drive on the road today, are you modeling Christian humility?

Are you displaying the mind of Christ by giving other cars the preference to be allowed to get into your lane? Philippians 2:3 says, "Do nothing from selfish or empty conceit, but with humility of mind regard one another as more important than yourselves; do not merely look out for your own personal interests, but also the interests of others."

If you're wondering how to display this Christ-like humility on the road, here is a word to the wise.

When you see that person trying to get over, rather than speeding up to keep them from getting in your lane, take some time to put them first. **It's okay!**

Today I will apply this wisdom in my life in the following ways:

_____

_____

To listen to this
Word to the Wise,
use your smart device
to scan the QR code!

February 26

The Whole Truth and Nothing but the Truth

I Timothy 3:15

The other day here at the College of Biblical Studies, one of our professors was speaking to a group of students about the role the College plays in equipping believers for life and ministry.

He referenced I Timothy 3:15 which says that believers, as the church, are "the pillar and support of the truth." In other words, believers are called to uphold God's truth in this world. And the College of Biblical Studies is equipping people to learn, live, and lead in the truth of God's Word.

If you've ever questioned what your purpose is, here is a word to the wise.

God has called you to learn the truth, live the truth, and to lead others to *the truth* of God's Word.

Today I will apply this wisdom in my life in the following ways:

_____

_____

To listen to this
Word to the Wise,
use your smart device
to scan the QR code!

Word to the Wise

February 27

Sins and Sinners

I John 4:20

We often hear that we should love the sinner and hate the sin.

C.S. Lewis said, "For a long time I used to think that was a silly, straw-splitting distinction. How can you hate what a man did and not hate the man? But years later it occurred to me that there was one man to whom I had been doing this all my life, namely, myself."

If you're having struggles loving others because of their sin, here is a word to the wise.

First John 4:20 says, "If someone says, 'I love God,' and hates his brother, he is a liar." If we can love our own sin and love ourselves, surely we can learn to love others despite of their sin.

Today I will apply this wisdom in my life in the following ways:

_____

_____

To listen to this
Word to the Wise,
use your smart device
to scan the QR code!

February 28

What Is Sin?

Philippians 4:8

Susanna Wesley defined "sin" to her young son, John Wesley, as follows: "Whatever weakens your reason, impairs the tenderness of your conscience, obscures your sense of God, and takes off the relish of spiritual things, that to you is sin."

Here's a question for you. Where do you put your focus? Here is a word to the wise.

Paul says in Philippians 4:8, "Finally, brothers and sisters, whatever is true, noble, right, pure, lovely, and admirable, if anything is excellent or praiseworthy, think on these things." In other words, when we keep our focus on the things that honor God, it keeps us from sin.

Today I will apply this wisdom in my life in the following ways:

_____

_____

To listen to this
Word to the Wise,
use your smart device
to scan the QR code!

What Are You Most Concerned With?

John 19:28

What do you think Christ was most concerned with during His final moments on the cross?

In John 19, *to fulfill the Scriptures*, Jesus said, "I am thirsty." When Jesus had received sour wine, He said, "It is finished." He bowed His head and gave up His Spirit. To the very end, our Savior was focused on fulfilling the Word of God.

If you feel like your devotion could never measure up to Christ, here is a word to the wise.

Because Jesus fulfilled the Scriptures, we are no longer condemned for our sin or our faulty devotion. If you believe this, what are you most concerned about today?

Today I will apply this wisdom in my life in the following ways:

_____

_____

To listen to this
Word to the Wise,
use your smart device
to scan the QR code!

March 1

Time to Press "Pause"

Psalm 39:6

Have you noticed that with all the technological advancements it seems that we are busier than ever?

Most importantly, we have less time for real relationships. Life can become so hectic when traveling at warp speed. Unfortunately, at this speed, life begins to unravel quickly, leaving us totally on empty. Psalm 39:6 reminds us that all of our busy rushing ends in nothing.

If you feel that you are going nowhere fast, here is a word to the wise.

Take the time to press "pause." Pray and ask God to reorder your priorities, and start living a meaningful life.

Today I will apply this wisdom in my life in the following ways:

_____

_____

To listen to this
Word to the Wise,
use your smart device
to scan the QR code!

March 2

Better Than Sacrifice

I Samuel 15:22

Ravi Zacharias once said, "Only when holiness and worship meet can evil be conquered. For that, only the Christian message has the answer."

Does your worship result in a holy lifestyle? In I Samuel 15:22, it says, "Behold, to obey is better than sacrifice."

If you want your worship to result in holy living, here is a word to the wise.

Sunday morning worship prepares you for a week of holy living; however, it does not substitute for it. Worship is the match that lights a fire through pain, but walking in obedience provides the fuel with no shame.

Today I will apply this wisdom in my life in the following ways:

_____

_____

To listen to this
Word to the Wise,
use your smart device
to scan the QR code!

March 3

Where Are the Keys?

Proverbs 17:24

Do you ever feel like the key to life and the wisdom you really need to unlock your future is just beyond your grasp?

Proverbs 17:24 says, "Wisdom is in the presence of the one who has understanding, but the eyes of a fool are on the ends of the earth." The wisdom that we really need is not in some faraway place or in achieving some impossible dream.

Have you ever thought the answers you really need are far beyond your reach? Here is a word to the wise.

Take advantage of what God has put right in front of you – His Word, His people, His ministry, and prayer. You'll find that you've held the key that unlocks your future all along.

Today I will apply this wisdom in my life in the following ways:

_____

_____

To listen to this *Word to the Wise*, use your smart device to scan the QR code!

Word to the **Wise**

March 4

Mystery of Marriage

Ephesians 5:32-33

Many marriages end in divorce, not because of adultery or some moral failure, but for incompatibility.

Do you know that God seems to always put opposites together? Why? According to Ephesians 5:32-33, he says, "This is a profound mystery, but I am talking about Christ and the church. However, each one of you also must love his wife as he loves himself, and the wife must respect her husband."

If you're about to bail on your marriage for all the wrong reasons, here is a word to the wise.

Change your focus. Marriage is not solely designed for our happiness. Marriage is designed to conform us to the image of Christ.

Today I will apply this wisdom in my life in the following ways:

_____

_____

To listen to this
Word to the Wise,
use your smart device
to scan the QR code!

64

The Ugly Truth

James 4:1

Paul David Tripp says, "Sin causes us to desire ugly things, say hurtful things, and do wicked things."

In James 4:1 it says, "What is the source of quarrels and conflicts among you? Is not the source your pleasures that wage war in your members? You lust and do not have, so you commit murder. You are envious and cannot obtain. So you fight and quarrel."

If your sin is making you do things that look ugly, here is a word to the wise.

A lust is anything you want so badly that you're willing to sin to get it. The only way to stop this ugliness is to turn away from your sin and turn to Christ.

Today I will apply this wisdom in my life in the following ways:

_____

_____

To listen to this
Word to the Wise,
use your smart device
to scan the QR code!

March 6

Someone's Watching

Proverbs 20:12

John Wooden said, "The true test of a man's character is what he does when no one is watching."

No doubt that's true, but the Bible makes it clear that someone is *always* watching. Proverbs 20:12 reads, "The hearing ear and the seeing eye, the Lord has made them both." There is nothing that is done or said in private that escapes God's notice.

If you've never considered the reality of God's omniscience, here is a word to the wise.

Purpose to do and say nothing in private that you would be ashamed of if it were made public. Whether alone or with others, keep your eyes on Jesus because He's always watching everything that you do.

Today I will apply this wisdom in my life in the following ways:

_____

_____

To listen to this
Word to the Wise,
use your smart device
to scan the QR code!

March 7

Perseverance
I Timothy 4:16

Charles Spurgeon said, "By perseverance, the snail reached the ark."

Can you relate to that little snail that had such a long distance to go just to get delivered?

In I Timothy 4:16, Paul tells Timothy to "pay close attention to yourself and to your teaching, persevering in these things, for as you do this, you will ensure salvation for both yourself and for those who hear you."

If your Christian walk is growing thin, here is a word to the wise.

Focus on God's Word. His promises are true. Your faith does impact others. Yes, the road to salvation may be long, but the ride is well worth the wait.

Today I will apply this wisdom in my life in the following ways:

_____

_____

To listen to this
Word to the Wise,
use your smart device
to scan the QR code!

March 8

Jesus Never Abandons His Friends

II Timothy 4:16-17

Have you ever felt abandoned by those you thought were your friends?

The apostle Paul certainly did. At the end of his life he wrote, "At my first offense, no one supported me but all deserted me." Facing the likelihood of execution for his faith, many of Paul's friends vanished. So, how do you suppose he responded?

Here is a word to the wise.

Paul went on to say, "May it not be counted against them, but the Lord stood with me and strengthened me." Instead of holding a grudge, he cast himself fully upon Jesus. Are you feeling alone? Don't worry. Jesus never abandons His friends.

Today I will apply this wisdom in my life in the following ways:

_____

_____

To listen to this
Word to the Wise,
use your smart device
to scan the QR code!

March 9

People Pleasers

Mark 15:15

The problem with being a people pleaser is that sometimes it can keep us from doing what is right.

Let's take Pilate, the people pleaser, for example. Mark 15:15 says, "So, Pilate, wishing to satisfy the crowd, released Barabbas for them and handed Jesus over to be crucified." His desire to please people kept him from doing the right thing. He turned over Jesus, who was completely innocent, to be crucified and let a known criminal go free.

Are you a people pleaser? Here is a word to the wise.

Don't compromise your Christian values to please people. You just might be crucifying your faith in Jesus.

Today I will apply this wisdom in my life in the following ways:

_____

_____

To listen to this *Word to the Wise,* use your smart device to scan the QR code!

March 10

Watch Out! Don't Fall!

Revelation 12:11

Dr. Chuck Swindoll said, "Unless your convictions mean everything to you now, they will mean nothing to you in times of pressure."

Are you willing to die for the cause of Christ? Revelation 12:11 describes believers who overcame. It says that they have defeated Satan by the blood of the Lamb and by their testimony, and they did not love their lives so much that they were afraid to die.

If you seek to stand by what you believe, here is a word to the wise.

You'll never be willing to die for Christ until you are willing to live for Him. Make a decision to stand for Christ or be ready to fall for anything.

Today I will apply this wisdom in my life in the following ways:

_____

_____

To listen to this
Word to the Wise,
use your smart device
to scan the QR code!

March 11

Who's in Your Mirror?

Genesis 27

Have you ever heard the criticism that believers' lives are as big a mess as everyone else's?

Judging by the account in Genesis 27, there is some truth to that. Isaac was self-indulgent and partial to his unbelieving son, Esau. Rebecca convinced Jacob to deceive his father, and Jacob lied to get a blessing. It's easy to see *their* sin, but if we take a close look in the mirror, we may find a little of ourselves in them.

Here is a word to the wise.

Unfortunately, the tangled web of sin affects us all. Thank God for His grace in Jesus, and may that grace lead us to greater holiness as we learn to live for Him.

Today I will apply this wisdom in my life in the following ways:

_____

_____

To listen to this *Word to the Wise,* use your smart device to scan the QR code!

March 12

Turn the Flashlight On!

James 2; Matthew 5:14

Benjamin Franklin said, "Words may show a man's wit, but actions his meaning."

In the Bible, James says that faith without works is useless. One of the most perplexing things in our society today is that it is hard to tell Christians from non-Christians. Jesus tells us in Matthew 5 that we are the light of the world and our light should be seen.

Is your light shining? Here is a word to the wise.

In a dark world, people don't need to know that you have a flashlight. They need to know that it's working. Let the love of Christ shine through you so that others may see!

Today I will apply this wisdom in my life in the following ways:

_____

_____

To listen to this
Word to the Wise,
use your smart device
to scan the QR code!

March 13

Spiritually Dehydrated?

John 4:14

According to some sources, in one day 20 million work hours are consumed by people collecting water for their families, and every day the cycle begins again.

Jesus said in John 4:14, "Whoever drinks of the water that I will give him shall never thirst."

If you've never considered the effects of spiritual dehydration all around you, here is a word to the wise.

Think of the millions of hours people spend trying to quench their spiritual thirst. Tell others about Jesus and put an end to this cycle of futility. Jesus is the wellspring of eternal life.

Today I will apply this wisdom in my life in the following ways:

_____

_____

To listen to this
Word to the Wise,
use your smart device
to scan the QR code!

March 14

I'm Praying About That

I Thessalonians 5:17; James 1:22; 4:3

A famous missionary once said, "Prayer is good, but when used as a substitute for obedience, it's nothing but blatant hypocrisy."

Indeed, the Bible says, "Pray without ceasing." However, praying should never be used as an excuse to say no.

If you're still saying, "I'm gonna pray about that," but are really just stalling – here is a word to the wise.

The book of James says, "You ask and do not receive because you ask with wrong motives …"; and, "Prove yourselves doers of the Word and not merely hearers who delude themselves." Unlike those who use prayer as an excuse not to obey, let this be your practice – pray *and* obey!

Today I will apply this wisdom in my life in the following ways:

_____

_____

To listen to this
Word to the Wise,
use your smart device
to scan the QR code!

74

March 15

Open the Flood Gates!

John 7:38

Here at the College of Biblical Studies, we are seeing the Holy Spirit transform the lives of His people through the study of God's Word.

As Jesus said about the Holy Spirit in John 7, "He who believes in Me from his innermost being will flow rivers of living water." The world offers us the stagnant water from the spirit of this age: self-indulgence, self-gratification, and self-promotion. But the Spirit of God uses the Word of God to transform us.

If you're in need of spiritual refreshment, here is a word to the wise.

Prayerfully and diligently study the Word of God, and watch the floodgates of divine blessing flow!

Today I will apply this wisdom in my life in the following ways:

_____

_____

To listen to this
Word to the Wise,
use your smart device
to scan the QR code!

March 16

Think Before You Speak

Proverbs 17:28

Someone has aptly stated, "It takes two years to learn to talk and seventy years to learn to keep your mouth shut."

No doubt, all of us say things we regret, and once words are spoken, we can't unspeak them.

The next time you're wondering whether you should say something or not, here is a word to the wise.

Proverbs 17:28 says, "Even a fool, when he keeps silent, is considered wise. When he closes his lips, he is considered prudent." If your words are in keeping with God's Word and in love, then speak. If not, learn the lesson of a lifetime. *Keep your mouth shut.*

Today I will apply this wisdom in my life in the following ways:

_____

_____

To listen to this
Word to the Wise,
use your smart device
to scan the QR code!

March 17

Belt of Truth

Ephesians 6:14

Did you know that every day you are engaged in a war?

Ephesians 6 says that believers fight against spiritual forces of wickedness in the heavens. Are you ready for battle? A Roman soldier's belt was essential for his self-defense. It kept his clothing and equipment in order. Paul calls believers to put on the "belt of truth."

If you feel like your life is out of control, here is a word to the wise.

Truthfulness is the belt that keeps the rest of our lives in order. So, the next time the enemy throws an accusation your way, *tighten your belt* and **press on in the truth**!

Today I will apply this wisdom in my life in the following ways:

_____

_____

To listen to this
Word to the Wise,
use your smart device
to scan the QR code!

March 18

Mind of Christ

Philippians 2:5

George Barna once said, "The primary reason that people don't act like Jesus is because they don't think like Jesus."

How many of your family members would say that your actions remind them of Christ? You may ask, "How is that possible?" One word – *sacrifice*. Philippians 2:5 says, "Have this attitude in yourselves which is also in Christ Jesus."

If you truly want to be like Christ, here is a word to the wise.

Ask God to give you the mind of Christ. While Jesus had every right to be served, He chose to obey God the Father and to be treated as a slave even when it cost Him His earthly life.

Today I will apply this wisdom in my life in the following ways:

_____

_____

To listen to this
Word to the Wise,
use your smart device
to scan the QR code!

78

March 19

Parting the Red Sea

Psalm 78:42

When was the last time you considered the ten plagues in Israel's exodus from Egypt?

Some would have to go back to Sunday School memories and others to the Charlton Heston movie.

If you have forgotten that the blood, the flies, frogs, and hail are more than just stories, here is a word to the wise.

Psalm 78:42 calls us not to forget the Lord's power demonstrated by the deadly plagues of the Exodus. The God we serve is the same One who parted the Red Sea and delivered His people from their enemies. The next time you are standing at the bank of your Red Sea, don't forget what **He** can do.

Today I will apply this wisdom in my life in the following ways:

_____

_____

To listen to this
Word to the Wise,
use your smart device
to scan the QR code!

Word to the **Wise**

March 20

Phone Home
Genesis 5:24

Did you know that the Bible refers to a kind of extraterrestrial life?

Genesis Chapter 5 records the genealogy from Adam to Noah, and each generation ends with the phrase "and he died." There is one notable exception, however. Genesis 5:24 says Enoch walked with God and then he disappeared because God took him away. So what happened to Enoch?

Here is a word to the wise.

Enoch didn't die and he didn't remain in this world. God took him to show that there is life beyond this world of death. So, go ahead, phone home! There is eternal life for those who are new creatures in Christ.

Today I will apply this wisdom in my life in the following ways:

_____

_____

To listen to this
Word to the Wise,
use your smart device
to scan the QR code!

March 21

Secret Sins

Joshua 16-17

Have you heard the saying, "The little foxes spoil the vine"?

Well, in Joshua Chapters 16 and 17, God commanded the Israelites to drive out all the Canaanites. Unfortunately, instead of driving them out, they kept some of the Canaanites as servants. As a result, the Israelites eventually assimilated into the Canaanite culture and began worshiping idol gods.

Disobeying God's Word may begin as a small compromise, but can eventually lead to a catastrophic lifestyle.

Are you living a life without compromise? Here is a word to the wise.

Ask God to help you deal with your secret sins before they **spoil your Christian witness**.

Today I will apply this wisdom in my life in the following ways:

_____

_____

To listen to this
Word to the Wise,
use your smart device
to scan the QR code!

March 22

Under the Influence

Ephesians 5:18

Did you know that God wants you to live your life under the influence? Not with wine, of course, but with the Spirit.

In Ephesians 5, the apostle Paul commands us to "be filled with the Spirit," and then he goes on to list certain results and responsibilities we must pursue.

If you're wondering how a believer can be filled with the Spirit of God, here is a word to the wise.

Allow the Word of Christ to richly dwell within you. When we allow God's Word to control our thinking and actions, we are being filled with the Holy Spirit. So go ahead! Live under the influence – _of God_.

Today I will apply this wisdom in my life in the following ways:

_____

_____

To listen to this
Word to the Wise,
use your smart device
to scan the QR code!

March 23

The Past Is Passed!

Hebrews 11

Are you crippled by your past?

Did you know that the Bible is full of people who are known by their stigma?

But by their faith in God, they overcame their circumstances. For example, Rahab the prostitute: Her name appears in five different chapters of the Bible – and in every place except Matthew she is known as a prostitute. By trusting God with her life as she hid two of Joshua's spies, her name is placed in Hebrew 11 with Abraham, Isaac, and Jacob as one of those who represents the Hall of Faith.

Here is a word to the wise.

Take a lesson from Rahab. You can't undo your past, but you can decide how you will live **your** future.

Today I will apply this wisdom in my life in the following ways:

_____

_____

To listen to this
Word to the Wise,
use your smart device
to scan the QR code!

March 24

Wash Water

Genesis 49:11; John 2:1-11

Do you remember Jesus' first miracle? He turned water into wine.

Genesis 49:11 prophesied that when the Messiah comes, God's people would so prosper that you could use wine as wash water. Why isn't it so today?

Here is a word to the wise.

Shortly after He turned water into wine, Jesus predicted His own death and resurrection. Before He could rule as King, the Lord would be crucified to pay the penalty for our sin.

But because of His death and resurrection, we are guaranteed sinless abundance in God's kingdom. So, until His kingdom comes, use your wash water for clothes and save *your wine for communion.*

Today I will apply this wisdom in my life in the following ways:

_____

_____

To listen to this
Word to the Wise,
use your smart device
to scan the QR code!

84

March 25

Very Best

Luke 11:11-13

Ruth Bell Graham said, "God hasn't always answered my prayers. If He had, I would have married the wrong man several times."

Have you ever prayed for something and been disappointed in God's answer?

Here is a word to the wise.

Luke 11 says that the Father only gives good gifts to His children when they ask Him for something. In fact, He has given His Holy Spirit to you – who prays for you in accord with His perfect will.

So don't be disappointed when you don't get what you ask for. Remember, God knows what you need and will only give you the very best.

Today I will apply this wisdom in my life in the following ways:

_____

_____

To listen to this
Word to the Wise,
use your smart device
to scan the QR code!

Ant University

Proverbs 6:6

Do you think you can learn anything from an ant?

Proverbs 6 says, "Look to the ant. Study its ways and learn." Even small, seemingly insignificant creatures can accomplish much and glorify God.

Here is a word to the wise.

Ants teach us patience and humility as we try to rid our yard of them, and they also teach us a theology of work. God declares there are lessons to be learned from these tiny little creatures.

If you are in need of humility, patience, or even a strong work ethic, maybe it's time that you enrolled in Ant University.

Today I will apply this wisdom in my life in the following ways:

_____

_____

To listen to this
Word to the Wise,
use your smart device
to scan the QR code!

March 27

Praise the Father, Son, and Holy Spirit

I Peter 1:2

What difference does the doctrine of the Trinity make in our lives?

First Peter 1:2 reveals that the entirety of our salvation depends on it. Believers were "chosen according to the foreknowledge of God the Father, by the sanctifying work of the Spirit, to obey Jesus Christ and be sprinkled with His blood."

If you've been tempted to discount the importance of the Trinity, here is a word to the wise.

The Father planned our redemption; Christ purchased our redemption by His blood; and the Holy Spirit effectually applied that redemption to those who believe. Now, that's a reason to praise the one true God – Father, Son, and Holy Spirit! Amen.

Today I will apply this wisdom in my life in the following ways:

_____

_____

To listen to this
Word to the Wise,
use your smart device
to scan the QR code!

March 28

You Ain't Seen Nothing Yet!

Psalm 96:12

Have you ever looked around at the creation and marveled at its beauty?

Yet the beauty of this world is nothing to be compared with the beauty when the Lord comes back. Psalm 96:12 says that the field and all that is in it will rejoice and all the trees in the forest will sing for joy at His coming.

Here is a word to the wise.

The Lord is coming and will make all things new. Creation will be more glorious than we can imagine. The sights, the sounds, the colors, and shapes will be inexpressibly awesome. But best of all, Jesus will rule. Now, that's beautiful!

Today I will apply this wisdom in my life in the following ways:

_____

_____

To listen to this
Word to the Wise,
use your smart device
to scan the QR code!

March 29

Hold My Hand, Child

Isaiah 41:13

Sometimes children refuse to hold their parent's hand while crossing the road; however, parents insist because they can see how to avoid the dangers while making the journey.

God declared to Israel in Isaiah 41:13, "For I am the Lord your God who holds your right hand, who says to you, 'Do not fear. I will help you.'"

If you are insisting that you can make it through life's crossroads alone, here is a word to the wise.

Don't do it. Trust God. He, like a loving parent, will hold your hand to get you safely to the other side.

Today I will apply this wisdom in my life in the following ways:

_____

_____

To listen to this
Word to the Wise,
use your smart device
to scan the QR code!

Like Father, Like Son

Genesis 26; Romans 8:29

Remember the expression, "Like father, like son"?

In Genesis 26, much like his father had decades earlier, Isaac lied about his wife because he was afraid of a Philistine king.

The Bible makes it clear that we're not doomed to commit the same sins as our earthly parents, but if you're worried about repeating your parents' past mistakes, here is a word to the wise.

Romans 8:29 says that, as believers, we are predestined to be conformed to the image of Christ. Take heart, beloved, you are a child of God, so walk in the ways of your *heavenly* Father.

Today I will apply this wisdom in my life in the following ways:

_____

_____

To listen to this
Word to the Wise,
use your smart device
to scan the QR code!

March 31

Facebook Fatigue

2 John 12

How many hours do you spend on social media?

It is good to use various means of communication to honor Christ, see His glory proclaimed, and even encourage others, but there's no substitute for face-to-face fellowship with other believers.

If you're suffering from Facebook fatigue, here is a word to the wise.

If the apostle John were living today, his second epistle would sound something like this: "I have much more to say to you but I don't want to put it on Facebook or Twitter, so I hope to visit you soon and talk with you face-to-face. Then our joy will be full."

While a post on social media may be good, prayer in person is always better.

Today I will apply this wisdom in my life in the following ways:

_____

_____

To listen to this
Word to the Wise,
use your smart device
to scan the QR code!

April 1

Listen to Reproof

Proverbs 12:1

The Scriptures are filled with examples of those who hated reproof and paid dearly for their pride.

Proverbs 12:1 says, "Whoever loves discipline loves knowledge, but he who hates reproof is stupid."

If you find yourself going into defense mode when someone else is trying to instruct you, here is a word to the wise.

Let down your defense shield and embrace the friend who loves you enough to tell you the truth, and listen to their reproof. Why? One, God may be speaking through them; and two, they may keep you from looking really stupid.

Today I will apply this wisdom in my life in the following ways:

_____

_____

To listen to this
Word to the Wise,
use your smart device
to scan the QR code!

April 2

Liar, Lunatic, or Lord?

John 5:21

Have you ever met someone who agrees that Jesus was a good teacher but won't accept that He is God?

In John 5:21, Christ said, "Just as the Father raises the dead and gives them life, even so, the Son also gives life to whom He wishes." Such statements reveal that Jesus is either a liar, or a lunatic, or Lord.

But how can we help others understand the truth that Jesus is Lord? Here is a word to the wise.

Christ didn't push Himself on those who refused to believe. But in love, He warned them of the consequences of such unbelief. Prayerfully, graciously, and humbly call those around you to worship Him as the **Lord** of life.

Today I will apply this wisdom in my life in the following ways:

_____

_____

To listen to this
Word to the Wise,
use your smart device
to scan the QR code!

April 3

Poison Control Center

Ephesians 4:31

Are you holding onto resentment or anger and noticing that you're the only person suffering?

A wise person once said, "Unforgiveness is like drinking poison and expecting the other person to die from it." Ephesians 4:31 says, "Let all bitterness and wrath and anger and clamor and slander be put away from you, along with all malice. Be kind to one another, tenderhearted, forgiving each other."

Here is a word to the wise.

Unforgiveness is a poison and the only antidote for it is extending to others the forgiveness that Christ gave you. Will you extend that forgiveness to someone today?

Today I will apply this wisdom in my life in the following ways:

_____

_____

To listen to this
Word to the Wise,
use your smart device
to scan the QR code!

April 4

NOW Is the Time

Ephesians 2:5

What would happen if all Christians could unite and each commit to sharing the good news of Jesus Christ to at least one person?

In Ephesians 2:5, Paul reminds the church at Ephesus and us that God made us alive with Christ even when we were dead in transgressions.

Ready to make a difference? Here is a word to the wise.

Remember the acronym NOW: **N** – Name one person you know that needs to hear the gospel of Jesus Christ; **O** – opportunity; pray that God would provide the perfect opportunity; and **W** – witness; share how Christ has changed your life and commit to demonstrating His lovingkindness toward them as long as it takes. NOW, let's see what happens!

Today I will apply this wisdom in my life in the following ways:

_____

_____

To listen to this *Word to the Wise,* use your smart device to scan the QR code!

Word to the **Wise**

April 5

The Ultimate Necessity

Genesis 8:20

Do you ever feel like you have so much to get done that you don't really have time to spend with God in worship?

Imagine how Noah must have felt after the flood. But according to Genesis 8:20, rather than immediately setting out to settle the land or seeking provisions, Noah worshiped God. Before he got busy with the details of life, Noah would honor the Giver of life.

If you have been tempted to check your cell phone rather than call on God, here is a word to the wise.

Before you start your quest for the daily necessities, worship God. Why? Because God is your **ultimate** necessity.

Today I will apply this wisdom in my life in the following ways:

_____

_____

To listen to this
Word to the Wise,
use your smart device
to scan the QR code!

April 6

Spiritual Vision

II Corinthians 5:7

Do you wear glasses or contacts? Even if you don't, there is a good chance as you get older you will.

As we age, weakening eyes are just a symptom of getting older. To offset this, we use corrective lenses, take vitamins, and a few of us eat lots of carrots — whatever it takes to keep those eyes sharp.

What do you do to keep your spiritual eyes sharp? In II Corinthians 5:7, Paul says, "We walk by faith and not by sight."

If you want a strong faith, here is a word to the wise.

Read the Bible, pray fervently, and fellowship consistently. This will keep your spiritual eyes at 20/20.

Today I will apply this wisdom in my life in the following ways:

_____

_____

To listen to this
Word to the Wise,
use your smart device
to scan the QR code!

April 7

What's Best?

Jeremiah 42-43

It's been said, "Obedience is not just good for you; it's best for you."

In Jeremiah 42, the people asked the prophet to give them direction from God about what to do. They promised that whether it is pleasant or unpleasant they would obey the voice of the Lord. Sadly, in Chapter 43, after Jeremiah told them, they accused him of lying and refused to obey the word of the Lord.

If you have ever asked the Lord for wisdom, then disregarded the Word because you didn't like it, here is a word to the wise.

God's Word never fails, and because He is good, obedience to His Word is not just good for you, it is **best** for you!

Today I will apply this wisdom in my life in the following ways:

_____

_____

To listen to this
Word to the Wise,
use your smart device
to scan the QR code!

April 8

He Is Faithful!

Psalm 142:3

Are you guilty of trusting God only in the good times?

The Israelites sometimes trusted the Lord and stood on His promises, but they often wavered in their faith. In the Old Testament, they believed His promises and sang His praise, but soon they forgot what He had done and they didn't wait for His plan to unfold.

Are you being pressured to abandon God's plan? Here is a word to the wise.

Scripture teaches us to believe the promises of God. *He is faithful!* According to Psalm 142:3, it says, "When I am overwhelmed, You alone know the way I should turn." So, trust God's plan. It <u>always</u> works.

Today I will apply this wisdom in my life in the following ways:

____

____

To listen to this *Word to the Wise*, use your smart device to scan the QR code!

April 9

Mark of Faith
I Peter 1:8

It's been said, "Faith is the identifying mark of a Christian."

But the word "faith" seems to mean different things to different people. Often, faith is portrayed as something like wishful thinking – just believing something will happen if you believe hard enough, for long enough. So, what really is faith that identifies a Christian?

Here is a word to the wise.

First Peter 1:8 says, "Though you have not seen Christ, you love Him, and though you do not see Him now but believe in Him, you greatly rejoice with joy inexpressible." Don't settle for wishful thinking. The mark of saving faith is love for Jesus Christ.

Today I will apply this wisdom in my life in the following ways:

_____

_____

To listen to this
Word to the Wise,
use your smart device
to scan the QR code!

100

God's Approval, Not Man's

John 12:43

Christian recording artist Lecrae said, "If you live for people's approval, you will die from their rejection."

Whose approval is most important to you? Human beings' or God's? John 12:43 describes the Pharisees as those who love the approval of men rather than the approval of God.

If you seek people's approval more than God's, here is a word to the wise.

Man's approval is fickle and, in the case of the Pharisees, deadly. Make it your priority to seek the approval of the One who gives life instead of those who try to take it away.

Today I will apply this wisdom in my life in the following ways:

_____

_____

To listen to this
Word to the Wise,
use your smart device
to scan the QR code!

April 11

Justice in the Light of the Cross

I Peter 3:18

Philip Yancey said, "Any discussion of how pain and suffering fit into God's scheme ultimately leads back to the cross. The offender often cries for mercy and the victim often cries for justice. However, God resolved this tension with the cross."

First Peter 3:18 says, "For Christ also died for sins, once for all, the just for the unjust, so that He might bring us to God."

If you feel as though you have been unjustly treated, here is a word to the wise.

When we feel that we are being treated unfairly, rather than insisting on our rights, let us remember our Savior who surrendered His rights to bring God the most glory.

Today I will apply this wisdom in my life in the following ways:

_____

_____

To listen to this
Word to the Wise,
use your smart device
to scan the QR code!

You *Can* Take It with You

I Peter 1:3-4

Remember the old saying, "You can't take it with you"? The Bible actually says you *can* take it with you.

First Peter 1:3-4 confirms that when you are born again because of the resurrection of Christ, you obtain "an inheritance which is imperishable, undefiled, and will not fade away, reserved in heaven for you."

If you're feeling uneasy about your retirement nest egg, here is a word to the wise.

No matter how diversified your 401k, it will not last forever. But when you put your trust in Jesus, you are fully vested. He guarantees that your faith will result in eternal dividends!

Today I will apply this wisdom in my life in the following ways:

_____

_____

To listen to this
Word to the Wise,
use your smart device
to scan the QR code!

April 13

Who Killed Christ?

Isaiah 53:5; John 10:18

Many have asked, "Who really killed Christ?"

Isaiah 53 says, "The Lord was pleased to crush Him, putting Him to grief if He would render Himself as a guilt offering. He was wounded for our transgressions. He was crushed for our iniquities, and by scourging, we are healed."

So who really killed Christ? Jesus said in the Gospel of John, "No one takes it from Me, but I lay it down on My own accord."

Here is a word to the wise.

God crushed His Son, and His Son willingly laid down His life. Why? Out of unfathomable love, Christ died for **you**!

Today I will apply this wisdom in my life in the following ways:

_____

_____

To listen to this
Word to the Wise,
use your smart device
to scan the QR code!

April 14

Divine Accounting

Colossians 2:13-14

Did you know that the IRS has at least one thing in common with God? They both have a ledger of balances due.

According to Colossians 2:13-14, those outside of Christ have a certificate of debt that is legally binding before God.

If you have not trusted in Christ, what does your ledger balance say? Here is a word to the wise.

Unlike our obligation to the IRS, the believer's debt has been nailed to the cross and canceled. Our sins have been forgiven. While you still have to pay your taxes, if you accept Christ as your Savior, your ledger now reads, "Paid in full by the blood of the Lamb."

Today I will apply this wisdom in my life in the following ways:

_____

_____

To listen to this
Word to the Wise,
use your smart device
to scan the QR code!

April 15

Manna from Heaven

Exodus 16:4

Many Christians as they grow older worry about their financial security.

Yes, sometimes there is tension between prudence and whether or not God will provide, but the principal question is: Do you worry or are you content about your future?

While in the wilderness, the Israelites grumbled against God about His provision for them. God replied in Exodus 16 by raining down bread from heaven.

If you're worried or complaining about your future, here is a word to the wise.

God wanted more for His people than to fill their bellies. He wanted them to trust in Him in all situations. If you trust God with your eternal security, surely He can be trusted with your financial security.

Today I will apply this wisdom in my life in the following ways:

_____

_____

To listen to this
Word to the Wise,
use your smart device
to scan the QR code!

106

April 16

Tangled in Life's Thorns

John 16:33

Thomas Boston said, "Sin has turned the world from a paradise into a patch of thorns. There is no getting through without being scratched."

Jesus promised in John 16:33 even for believers, "In this world you will have tribulation, but take courage. I have overcome the world."

If you're feeling like you're entangled in life's thorns, here is a word to the wise.

Because Jesus has risen, He has defeated death and overcome the world. His crown of thorns guarantees that while the barbs of this world may hurt us, they will ultimately never ever destroy us.

Today I will apply this wisdom in my life in the following ways:

_____

_____

To listen to this
Word to the Wise,
use your smart device
to scan the QR code!

April 17

Look to Jesus and Live

Matthew 27:44; Mark 15:32; Luke 23:39-43

Have you ever wondered if God would really forgive you?

The Bible says there were two thieves crucified alongside Christ, both hurling abuse at Him. One of the thieves later had a change of heart. He uttered this simple prayer: "Jesus, remember me when you come into Your kingdom." Jesus promised, "Today, you shall be with Me in paradise." Though he had mocked Christ just hours before, this dying man looked to Jesus for mercy.

If you think you've exceeded the limit of God's forgiveness, here is a word to the wise.

No matter how you may have sinned in the past, even you can repent. Look to Jesus and live.

Today I will apply this wisdom in my life in the following ways:

_____

_____

To listen to this
Word to the Wise,
use your smart device
to scan the QR code!

April 18

Blessings of Forgiveness

Psalm 32:1

Sinclair Ferguson said, "Those who are most conscious of forgiveness are invariably those who have been most acutely convicted of their sin."

Psalm 32:1 reads, "How blessed is he whose transgression is forgiven, whose sin is covered."

If you've forgotten how blessed you really are, here is a word to the wise.

If you've trusted in Christ, all of your sins, past, present, and future, are completely dealt with through His cross. Take time to remember what you really deserve; then praise God for His ongoing blessing of forgiveness through Jesus Christ.

Today I will apply this wisdom in my life in the following ways:

_____

_____

To listen to this
Word to the Wise,
use your smart device
to scan the QR code!

April 19

Because He Lives

I Corinthians 15:17-22

Some argue that it doesn't matter if Jesus was literally resurrected from the dead.

The apostle Paul wrote in I Corinthians 15, "If Christ has not been raised, your faith is worthless. You are still in your sins ... If we have hope in Christ in this life only, we are of all men most to be pitied."

Does the resurrection really matter? Here is a word to the wise.

Your eternal future, as well as your temporal tomorrow, is based on Christ's victory over death. Jesus is not just a good example. Because He lives, those who trust in Him will live now **and forever!**

Today I will apply this wisdom in my life in the following ways:

_____

_____

To listen to this
Word to the Wise,
use your smart device
to scan the QR code!

April 20

Spare No Expense

Genesis 23

Did you know that price gouging for a cemetery plot is not a new phenomenon?

In Genesis 23, Abraham paid what seems to be an exorbitant price for a field so he could bury his beloved Sarah.

Why did he do it? Here is a word to the wise.

He was not caught up in the emotion of the moment, but he believed in the resurrection and God's promise to give him the land. The purchase would stand as a testimony to the hope of the resurrection.

The Bible isn't calling you to overpay for a casket, headstone, or a tomb. God *is* calling you to spare no expense at proclaiming your hope in the resurrection and His faithful promises to you!

Today I will apply this wisdom in my life in the following ways:

_____

_____

To listen to this
Word to the Wise,
use your smart device
to scan the QR code!

April 21

You Complete Me

Colossians 2:10

Do you ever feel that you need something more than faith in Christ to be really spiritual?

According to Colossians 2, in Christ all believers have been made complete by faith. There is no need for a special vision or to abstain from certain foods to be more spiritual.

If you're relying on your experiences, your religious activity, or even your discipline in your relationship with God to be complete, here is a word to the wise.

Unlike those who trust in religious activities or personal experiences, glory in Christ Jesus alone and put no confidence in the flesh. Christ is the One who makes us complete. He is all we need.

Today I will apply this wisdom in my life in the following ways:

_____

_____

To listen to this
Word to the Wise,
use your smart device
to scan the QR code!

April 22

Eating Rat Poison

Romans 6:23

Engaging in sin is like a rat that slowly eats poison because it thinks it tastes good without recognizing that it was designed to kill it.

Did you know that sin is not only hurtful, it is deadly? Romans 6:23 says, "For the wages of sin is death, but the gift of God is eternal life in Christ Jesus our Lord." Living in sin may temporarily feel good, but it will demand a bigger payout that you cannot afford.

If you're looking for a way out, here is a word to the wise.

God has given you the free gift of life through Christ Jesus. Ask Him today and start living!

Today I will apply this wisdom in my life in the following ways:

_____

_____

To listen to this
Word to the Wise,
use your smart device
to scan the QR code!

April 23

What's Your Relationship Status?

I sometimes hear people say, "If God will do a miracle, maybe I'll believe in Him."

"If He would allow me to hit the lottery or cure my family member from a chronic disease, then I'll put my trust in Him."

Have you ever said these words? Do you need a miracle in order to trust Christ? In the Bible, Jesus performed many incredible miracles in His own hometown of Capernaum. Yet, many never believed and today the three towns where Christ performed most of His miracles are all uninhabited.

Here is a word to the wise.

Miracles alone won't bring you to faith in Christ. The most critical issue in life is your relationship with Jesus. Here is a question for you. What is the status of <u>your</u> relationship?

Today I will apply this wisdom in my life in the following ways:

_____

_____

To listen to this
Word to the Wise,
use your smart device
to scan the QR code!

April 24

I Did It!

One day while rushing to church, I stopped to get gas and accidentally locked my eighteen-month-old son in the car.

When he figured out that he was locked in and I was locked out, he started to cry. The only way for me to get in was to encourage him to unlock his belt, get out of his seat, climb over the front seat, and then press the right button and then let me in. In other words, I needed a miracle. Needless to say, that's exactly what happened. He opened the door and he said with tears in his eyes, "Daddy, I did it!"

Here is a word to the wise.

Do you ever feel like you're locked in and can't get out to enjoy life? Try Jesus today and then you can say, "I did it!"

Today I will apply this wisdom in my life in the following ways:

_____

_____

To listen to this
Word to the Wise,
use your smart device
to scan the QR code!

April 25

Get Going!

Colossians 4:3

The other day here at the College of Biblical Studies, a group of about fifteen students, along with staff, joined hands to praise God and seek boldness in taking His Word to the world.

The apostle Paul prayed in Colossians 4:3 that God would open the door for the Word so that he could speak forth the mystery of Christ.

If you sometimes feel timid about sharing your faith, here is a word to the wise.

Praying with others for God to sovereignly prepare opportunities to witness is one way to prepare yourself for those opportunities as they arise. Don't just think about it. Gather with other believers and pray, and then go out and proclaim it!

Today I will apply this wisdom in my life in the following ways:

_____

_____

To listen to this
Word to the Wise,
use your smart device
to scan the QR code!

April 26

Others Are Watching

Acts 16:22-25

What is your reaction when people oppose your faith?

In Acts 16, Paul and Silas were beaten with rods, thrown in prison, and their feet chained in stocks. Their response was surprising to most. They chose to pray and sing hymns of praise to God. Later, the jailer came to Christ in faith because of their testimony.

If you are more prone to anger than praise, here is a word to the wise.

Like the guard that night, the world is watching how believers respond to suffering and persecution. Watch how you respond in a crisis. The salvation of others may be at stake.

Today I will apply this wisdom in my life in the following ways:

_____

_____

To listen to this
Word to the Wise,
use your smart device
to scan the QR code!

April 27

Are You a Doubting Thomas?

John 20:28-29

Do you remember Doubting Thomas' reaction to finally seeing the resurrected Christ? He said, "My Lord and my God!" Jesus replied, "Because you have seen Me, you have believed. Blessed are those who have not seen Me and yet believe."

If you wish you could be blessed by some extraordinary experience, here is a word to the wise.

The most miraculous experience of Christ is the gift of faith. You believe even though you haven't seen Him personally. Divine blessings come from trusting Jesus, not from some mystical experience. When you **walk by faith**, you are truly blessed!

Today I will apply this wisdom in my life in the following ways:

_____

_____

To listen to this
Word to the Wise,
use your smart device
to scan the QR code!

April 28

Drop That Load!

Philippians 4:13

Are you exhausted? Are the stresses of life weighing you down? Have you ever felt like giving up?

If someone asks you, "How do you get through the rough stuff?" Or, "What do you do to get the weight lifted?" What do you say?

Unfortunately, many Christians go through life without knowing the power available in Christ.

Are you tired of carrying that load? Here is a word to the wise.

Philippians 4:13 says, "I can do all things through Christ who strengthens me." In the Christian walk, we can never handle all the pressures of life. Only God can do that. Let Jesus be your spiritual load carrier, and let it go!

Today I will apply this wisdom in my life in the following ways:

_____

_____

To listen to this
Word to the Wise,
use your smart device
to scan the QR code!

April 29

Who Can Stand Against Us?

Romans 8:31

Do you ever feel like the entire world is against you?

Romans 8:31 says, "If God is for us, who can ever be against us?"

If you're letting others get the best of you, here is a word to the wise.

God has a plan for you as a believer. He sent His own Son to save you and He will never let anything keep you from fulfilling the purpose He has for you.

So take courage! Nothing can separate you from the love of God in Christ and no one can stand against Him. You know the final outcome of this battle. You know how this story ends: With Christ, you have already won.

Today I will apply this wisdom in my life in the following ways:

_____

_____

To listen to this
Word to the Wise,
use your smart device
to scan the QR code!

April 30

Don't Give Up!

II Corinthians 4:17

Do you ever feel like the trials of this life are a bit too much?

Most of us have at some point. The apostle Paul reminds us as believers, in II Corinthians 4:17, "Momentary light affliction is producing for us an eternal weight of glory far beyond all comparison."

If you're feeling like your afflictions are neither light nor momentary, here is a word to the wise.

The heavier the trial and the longer it lasts, when you keep on trusting Christ, it produces an infinitely greater and longer-lasting result of glory in the age to come. Don't give up. Your Deliverer is coming and your reward will be worth it all!

Today I will apply this wisdom in my life in the following ways:

_____

_____

To listen to this *Word to the Wise,* use your smart device to scan the QR code!

May 1

Finish the Race

Acts 20:24

Every year at graduation, students often suffer from what is commonly called "senioritis."

This is a tendency to run out of steam as the race is about to finish. Sad to say, many never finish.

Many Christians have senioritis. They give up on their children, their job, and their ministry. And some, in frustration, give up on life. Where are you in the race that God has given you?

If you are on the verge of giving up, here is a word to the wise.

Don't let senioritis get the best of you. In Acts 20:24, Paul calls you to finish the race and complete the task the Lord Jesus has given to you.

Today I will apply this wisdom in my life in the following ways:

_____

_____

To listen to this
Word to the Wise,
use your smart device
to scan the QR code!

May 2

More Than a Feeling

Philippians 2:2

Have you ever asked God to give you more love?

God sometimes places unlovable people in our life to teach us the real meaning of love. God made all people different, but we must maintain the same love by loving with the same mind as Christ.

Paul says in Philippians 2:2, "Make my joy complete by being of the same mind, maintaining the same love."

If you desire to love more biblically, here is a word to the wise.

Remember, loving others is more than just a feeling. It is a commitment to be more like Christ. Ask God to give you the ability to love others like He loves you.

Today I will apply this wisdom in my life in the following ways:

_____

_____

To listen to this
Word to the Wise,
use your smart device
to scan the QR code!

May 3

What's Your Legacy?

Proverbs 11:29

Are you a cause of rejoicing for your family or a cause of trouble?

Our outlook on life, our moods, and our worries can either bless or burden others and ourselves. Proverbs 11:29 says, "He who troubles his own house will inherit the wind."

If you sense your attitudes and actions have been more disagreeable than delightful, here is a word to the wise.

Don't let sinful attitudes become your legacy. Purpose today to be a blessing to those around you. Ask God to produce the fruit of His Spirit in you. It's your choice. You can inherit the emptiness of the wind, or eternal wealth by pointing your family to Christ.

Today I will apply this wisdom in my life in the following ways:

_____

_____

To listen to this *Word to the Wise*, use your smart device to scan the QR code!

May 4

Too Great a Debt

II Samuel 11

J. C. Ryle said, "People fall in private long before they fall in public."

One of the difficult realities for Christians is that we forget God sees everything. David hid his deep lust for Bathsheba in his heart long before he was confronted by Nathan. Unfortunately, it was too late when it became public.

Are you hiding any secret sin in your heart? Here is a word to the wise.

Sin will make you hide and run away. Sin will make you lie and make up words to say. But before it's done, sin will create a debt that you will not be able to pay.

Today I will apply this wisdom in my life in the following ways:

_____

_____

To listen to this
Word to the Wise,
use your smart device
to scan the QR code!

Compromise Kills

Hebrews 12:4

Historians report that artists in the early church were tempted to make their living from the production of idols.

Some justified their actions by saying they must live. The early church pastor Tertullian responded with a probing question: "Must you live?" Hebrews 12:4 exhorts believers not to grow weary in living for Christ. It says, "You have not yet resisted to the point of shedding blood in your striving against sin."

If you feel like compromising your faith is the only option in some situations, here is a word to the wise.

Compromise kills, but the one who would rather lose his life than sin will *truly* live.

Today I will apply this wisdom in my life in the following ways:

_____

_____

To listen to this
Word to the Wise,
use your smart device
to scan the QR code!

May 6

In God We Trust

John 6:40; Hebrews 13:5

There has been some talk about removing "In God We Trust" from our U.S. currency.

In a world filled with broken promises, if we can't trust God, whom can we trust?

D. L. Moody once said, "God never made a promise that was too good to be true." Here are two of God's promises: 1) "Everyone who looks to the Son and believes in Him shall have eternal life." And 2) Jesus said, "I will never leave you nor forsake you."

If you're looking for someone you can trust, here is a word to the wise.

Unlike others you meet, God cannot lie. He never makes a promise that He will not keep. Yes, in God we *do* trust, and you can take *that* to the bank.

Today I will apply this wisdom in my life in the following ways:

_____

_____

To listen to this
Word to the Wise,
use your smart device
to scan the QR code!

May 7

Sweet Tooth for Sin?

Hebrews 3:13

Have you ever heard the saying, "Sin will take you farther than you want to go, keep you longer than you want to stay, and cost you more than you're willing to pay"?

Sin is like cotton candy. It looks like it will satisfy you, but in the end, it's nothing but sugar-coated air that nourishes no one. The Bible warns us that we should beware of how deceitful sin is. In Hebrews 3:13, it says, "But encourage one another day after day as long as it is called today so that none of you will be hardened by the deceitfulness of sin."

If you're developing a sweet tooth for sin, here is a word to the wise.

Put down the cotton candy! God's Word is sweeter than honey in your mouth.

Today I will apply this wisdom in my life in the following ways:

_____

_____

To listen to this
Word to the Wise,
use your smart device
to scan the QR code!

May 8

Who Can Stand Against Us?

Ecclesiastes 7:21-22

Have you ever noticed that those who are most outspoken seem to be most easily offended by what other people say?

The *Message Bible* says in Ecclesiastes 7:21, "Don't eavesdrop on the conversation of others. What if the gossip is about you and you'd rather not hear it. You've done that a few times, haven't you? Said things behind someone's back you wouldn't say to his face?"

If you're tempted to be easily offended by what others say, here is a word to the wise.

When you overhear someone criticizing you, take Solomon's advice. Let it go. When it comes to your critics, remember, time and truth will eventually vindicate your character.

Today I will apply this wisdom in my life in the following ways:

_____

_____

To listen to this
Word to the Wise,
use your smart device
to scan the QR code!

May 9

Praise God for His Patience

I Timothy 1:15

Dr. John Piper said, "The work of sin and Satan go on in our day. God permits this within bounds to expose the exceeding sinfulness of sin and to magnify the greatness of His mercy in saving sinners like us."

In I Timothy 1:15, Paul says that Christ Jesus came into the world to save sinners.

Are you wrestling with your sins prior to salvation? Here is a word to the wise.

Praise God for His patience! If you have repented for your past sins, thank Him today for His tender mercies.

Today I will apply this wisdom in my life in the following ways:

_____

_____

To listen to this
Word to the Wise,
use your smart device
to scan the QR code!

May 10

Live It Out!

Ephesians 6:14

Which do you think the devil fears more? Those who shout at him or those who shut him up by living their lives with integrity?

In Ephesians 6:14, Paul calls believers to put on the "breastplate of righteousness." The breastplate protected a soldier's vital organs.

If you're shouting at the devil but feel like he's not really listening, here is a word to the wise.

It is essential that we are protected against the enemy's attack. So by grace, live out what God says is right rather than shout at the one who wants to do you wrong.

Today I will apply this wisdom in my life in the following ways:

_____

_____

To listen to this
Word to the Wise,
use your smart device
to scan the QR code!

God's 360° Assessment

Psalm 139:23

Most successful leaders at some point will have someone conduct a 360° assessment on their management or leadership ability.

This process involves surveying the leader's direct reports, peers, and even supervisors, confidentially to get feedback to help the leader become more effective.

Did you know that the Bible has a plan to make you a better Christian? In Psalm 139:23, David says, "Search me, O God, and know my heart. Try me and know my anxious thoughts. And see if there be any hurtful way in me, and lead me in the everlasting way."

Here is a word to the wise.

If you desire to be a better Christian, ask God to give **His** 360° assessment on you today!

Today I will apply this wisdom in my life in the following ways:

_____

_____

To listen to this
Word to the Wise,
use your smart device
to scan the QR code!

May 12

Impossibility or Opportunity?

Ezekiel 37

Chuck Swindoll said, "We are all faced with a series of great opportunities brilliantly disguised as impossible situations."

The prophet Ezekiel was faced with an opportunity to trust and obey the Lord with what seemed to be an insurmountable task. By way of a vision, God commanded him to preach to dry bones.

If you fail to see the opportunities in difficult situations in your life, here is a word to the wise.

Ezekiel obeyed and God brought life out of death. So the next time you're faced with the impossible, take advantage of the great opportunity. Trust God and do what He says, because He is faithful to do all that He has promised!

Today I will apply this wisdom in my life in the following ways:

_____

_____

To listen to this
Word to the Wise,
use your smart device
to scan the QR code!

May 13

Praise the Lord!

Psalm 117

At the College of Biblical Studies, we are equipping men and women with the tools to properly understand and apply the Scriptures to their own lives and proclaim the truth to others.

We believe that this will ultimately result in praise to God for His wondrous glory and love. Psalm 117 says, "Praise the Lord, all nations. Laud Him all people, for His lovingkindness is great toward us and the truth of the Lord is everlasting. Praise the Lord."

If it's been a while since you praised the Lord, here is a word to the wise.

God has revealed Himself and His love through the Scriptures. Take time *today* and praise the Lord.

Today I will apply this wisdom in my life in the following ways:

_____

_____

To listen to this
Word to the Wise,
use your smart device
to scan the QR code!

May 14

Billboard of Love

John 13:35

So many times, as Christians we try to win nonbelievers to Christ by our knowledge of the Bible.

At other times, we try to bring friends to Christ by telling them what we are doing with our good works.

Are you guilty of just talking the talk? John 13:35 says, "By this, all men will know that you are My disciples if you have love for one another."

If your evangelistic efforts are coming short, here is a word to the wise.

According to Jesus, the best advertisement for discipleship is not your theology or works, but **your love**. Today, may you be a billboard of love for all to see!

Today I will apply this wisdom in my life in the following ways:

_____

_____

To listen to this *Word to the Wise,* use your smart device to scan the QR code!

May 15

Get to Work!

Philippians 2:12-13

Did you know that the Bible teaches believers to work at their Christian life?

Paul says in Philippians 2:12-13, "Work out your salvation with fear and trembling for it is God who is at work in you, both to will and to work His good pleasure."

If you ever wondered how God's control over all things and your obedience are related, here is a word to the wise.

When you choose to live out your faith in obedience to God's Word, God's grace is at work, giving you the willingness and strength to obey. So, get to work! Live by faith, and praise God because it's all about *His* grace.

Today I will apply this wisdom in my life in the following ways:

_____

_____

To listen to this
Word to the Wise,
use your smart device
to scan the QR code!

Good Company

Proverbs 13:20

Many have said, "Show me a man's friends, and I'll tell you what kind of man he is."

The reality is, whoever or whatever you spend most of your time with will inevitably shape your character. What do your relationships say about you? Proverbs 13:20 says, "He who walks with wise men will be wise, but the companion of fools will suffer harm."

If your relationships are destroying your character, here is a word to the wise.

Walk with the wise. Spend time with Jesus and those who honor Him and you'll always be in good company!

Today I will apply this wisdom in my life in the following ways:

_____

_____

To listen to this
Word to the Wise,
use your smart device
to scan the QR code!

Word to the **Wise**

May 17

Worship and Wallets

Matthew 6:21

Remember that old hymn, "When I Survey the Wondrous Cross"?

It says, "Were the whole realm of nature mine, That were a gift far too small; Love so amazing, so divine, Demands my soul, my life, my all." Sometimes we sing such words while fumbling in our pockets for the smallest coin for the offering.

If you spend more at Starbucks than in the service of the gospel, here is a word to the wise.

Jesus said in Matthew 6:21, "Where your treasure is there your heart will be also." For those of us who love Christ, there should be a connection between our **worship** and our **wallets**.

Today I will apply this wisdom in my life in the following ways:

_____

_____

To listen to this
Word to the Wise,
use your smart device
to scan the QR code!

138

May 18

Good Pharisee or Good Samaritan?

James 2:13

Roger Ellsworth said, "One of the saddest dimensions of our day is that so many Christians are absorbed with seminars, charts, notebooks, study groups, and discipling techniques that they don't have the time to bake a cake, send a card, or mow the grass for the sick, the elderly, and the lonely."

If this sounds like you, here is a word to the wise.

James 2:13 says, "For judgment will be merciless to the one who shows no mercy. Mercy triumphs over judgment." Focus your efforts on showing unbelievers what Christianity *is* rather than constantly reminding them of what it's *against*.

Ellsworth concluded by saying, "It's easy to be a very good Pharisee while the world cries for a Good Samaritan."

Today I will apply this wisdom in my life in the following ways:

_____

_____

To listen to this
Word to the Wise,
use your smart device
to scan the QR code!

May 19

Stairway to Heaven

Genesis 28; John 1:51

The tallest staircase in the world has 11,674 steps and rises over a mile in elevation.

As high as it goes, it still falls woefully short of heaven. In Genesis 28, Jacob dreamed of a stairway that reached to heaven. Jesus used the same language of Himself in John 1:51 to reveal that *He* is the divine stairway between God and man.

If your life sometimes feels like you're trying to go up on a down escalator, here is a word to the wise.

You can't buy your way to heaven or build a stairway through your own efforts. Rest in Jesus. His love will lead you **all the way to glory**!

Today I will apply this wisdom in my life in the following ways:

_____

_____

To listen to this
Word to the Wise,
use your smart device
to scan the QR code!

Providence, Prayer, and Preference

Genesis 24

Some have said, "Coincidence is God's way of remaining anonymous."

In Genesis 24, Abraham's servant prayed for God's guidance to help him find a wife for Isaac. Events unfolded as he had prayed, and Rebekah agreed to travel hundreds of miles to marry a man she had never met. Wow!

How can you account for the so-called coincidences of life? Here is a word to the wise.

Providence, prayer, and personal preferences are working together to accomplish God's plan. So don't worry about the unknown. Pray for God's will! Embrace God's priorities! And trust God's providence!

Today I will apply this wisdom in my life in the following ways:

_____

_____

To listen to this
Word to the Wise,
use your smart device
to scan the QR code!

May 21

S.O.S.

Isaiah 40

Sometimes in life we go through wilderness experiences.

In the Old Testament, wilderness experiences are pictured as a place of testing. It is also a place where God demonstrates His grace is sufficient.

Are you going through a wilderness experience? Here is a word to the wise.

Our problems may be bigger than we are, but they're not more powerful than God's Word. Isaiah 40 says, "Clear the way, for the Lord is in the wilderness." We can focus on our problems and be discouraged, or we can focus on God and be encouraged. So clear the way for the Lord to rescue you – even in the wilderness!

Today I will apply this wisdom in my life in the following ways:

_____

_____

To listen to this
Word to the Wise,
use your smart device
to scan the QR code!

There Is a Purpose

Hebrews 12:2

Dr. Bob Pyne offers a great point on how Christ's life sufferings can give hope.

It is true that Jesus knew His sufferings would be temporary and that He would soon be restored to glory. However, it's not true that our own sufferings are utterly pointless and absurd. A high view of the providence of God affirms that all things ultimately have a purpose, even evil acts which appear to be completely senseless.

Hebrews 12:2 says, "For the joy set before Him, He endured the cross, despising the shame."

Are you going through suffering right now that seems pointless? Here is a word to the wise.

Like Jesus, we can have hope in the midst of our pain, because Jesus Himself is our hope!

Today I will apply this wisdom in my life in the following ways:

_____

_____

To listen to this *Word to the Wise,* use your smart device to scan the QR code!

May 23

How to Persevere with Joy

James 1:5

Vance Havner said, "If you lack knowledge, go to school. If you lack wisdom, get on your knees."

It is one thing to know that God is working in our trouble, but quite another to know how to have joy in the midst of it. James 1:5 says, "If any of you lacks wisdom, let him ask of God, and it will be given to him."

If you're struggling to endure your trial, here is a word to the wise.

Ask God for wisdom in how to persevere with joy. Unlike those who pray and expect God to answer their way, ask God for wisdom. Then trust and obey!

Today I will apply this wisdom in my life in the following ways:

_____

_____

To listen to this
Word to the Wise,
use your smart device
to scan the QR code!

Be a Blessing!

Genesis 30:27

Anne Graham Lotz has said about her mother, "Anybody who was in her presence was blessed to be there."

In Genesis 30:27, even Jacob's conniving father-in-law said to him, "The Lord has blessed me on your account." Are others blessed by God because of your presence in their lives?

Here is a word to the wise.

Your unbelieving boss will be blessed by God as you do your work as unto the Lord. Your unbelieving neighbor will be blessed as you build a relationship for Christ's sake. Some may try to take advantage of you, but the Lord will ultimately protect you. So, what are you waiting for? To be blessed, be a blessing!

Today I will apply this wisdom in my life in the following ways:

_____

_____

To listen to this
Word to the Wise,
use your smart device
to scan the QR code!

May 25

Built to Last

Did you know that Israel is filled with ancient ruins?

Many of these marvelous places were built by King Herod the Great. King Herod built these things to honor himself, thinking they would last forever.

Peter on the other hand sacrificed his life for furthering the name of Christ.

Here is a word to the wise.

As you journey through life, what are you building? When the final chapter of your life is written, will your life's work crumble to dust or last through all eternity? Take a note from the old famous hymn that says, "Only one life will soon be past, And only what's done for Christ will last!"

Today I will apply this wisdom in my life in the following ways:

_____

_____

To listen to this
Word to the Wise,
use your smart device
to scan the QR code!

May 26

More Privileged Than the Prophets

I Peter 1:10-12

Have you ever wished God would speak to you like He did to Moses or Elijah?

Actually, I Peter 1:10-12 says that the Old Testament prophets longed to know what *you* know as a New Testament believer. The Bible is a more complete and perfect revelation from God than any vision, dream, or temporary audible voice. If that's true, then why do we so often wish we could have a special word from God?

Here is a word to the wise.

Stop looking for some mystical event and start making time to seek God in His Word. If you do, you will discover truth that the prophets only dreamed about knowing.

Today I will apply this wisdom in my life in the following ways:

_____

_____

To listen to this
Word to the Wise,
use your smart device
to scan the QR code!

May 27

Praying for Holy Hatred

Proverbs 8:13

Dr. John Piper said, "The self that loves sin has died. The new self is not yet perfect. It sins but it does not make peace with sin. It hates sin. It confesses sin and makes war on sin."

Sin is not something we should make peace with. We must hate it with a holy hatred.

If you are too comfortable in your sin, here is a word to the wise.

Proverbs 8:13 says, "The fear of the Lord is to hate evil." Do you love sin more than you love Jesus? Pray today for a holy hatred of the sins that you love the most.

Today I will apply this wisdom in my life in the following ways:

_____

_____

To listen to this
Word to the Wise,
use your smart device
to scan the QR code!

May 28

Repentance or Relief?

Jeremiah 34

Martin Luther said, "Repentance which is occupied with thoughts of peace is hypocrisy."

Peace *with God* should be the motivating factor in our repentance, but in Jeremiah 34, the Lord rebuked Israel for trying to find relief from their difficulty without true repentance.

If you struggle to know the difference between true repentance and the deceptive desire for temporal peace, here is a word to the wise.

Do what the Lord calls you to do, even if you find no relief from your troubles in this life. While merely seeking relief is not repentance, repentance will result in eternal relief – *peace with God*.

Today I will apply this wisdom in my life in the following ways:

_____

_____

To listen to this
Word to the Wise,
use your smart device
to scan the QR code!

May 29

Are You Having Fun Yet?

II Peter 2:20

Peter Marshall said, "We are all too Christian to really enjoy sinning and all too fond of sin to really enjoy Christianity."

It says in II Peter 2:20, when people escape the wickedness of this world by knowing our Lord and Savior Jesus Christ and then get entangled and enslaved by sin again, they are worse off than before.

If your sin is out of control, here is a word to the wise.

The Holy Spirit will not allow us to enjoy sinning. So face it – your days of enjoying sin are over. Confess those secret sins to Him today, and enjoy the freedom of your salvation!

Today I will apply this wisdom in my life in the following ways:

_____

_____

To listen to this
Word to the Wise,
use your smart device
to scan the QR code!

No More Shame

Psalm 51

Have you ever been ashamed over your sin?

If so, that's good news. In Psalm 51, David prayed, "Cleanse me from my sin for I know my transgressions. A broken and contrite heart, O God, You will not despise."

Are you convicted over your sin? Here is a word to the wise.

Don't shift the blame or try to justify yourself. Pray like David. "Be gracious to me, O God, according to Your lovingkindness. Blot out my transgressions." Because of Jesus, God does indeed blot out the sins of those who trust in Him. No more shame. Now that's good news!

Today I will apply this wisdom in my life in the following ways:

_____

_____

To listen to this
Word to the Wise,
use your smart device
to scan the QR code!

May 31

I Surrender All?

Romans 12:1

I think if most Christians were honest, they would sing the famous hymn, "I Surrender All," like this: *"I surrender fifty percent. I surrender twenty-five percent. Fifteen percent to Thee, my blessed Savior, I surrender five percent."*

If this sounds like your Christian commitment, here is a word to the wise.

Romans 12:1 says, "Therefore, I urge you, brethren, by the mercies of God to present your bodies a living and holy sacrifice." Too often we want to have one foot in the world and the other foot with God. If you aim to follow Him, make a commitment today to completely surrender **all**.

Today I will apply this wisdom in my life in the following ways:

_____

_____

To listen to this
Word to the Wise,
use your smart device
to scan the QR code!

June 1

Let It Out – Sing to Him with All Your Heart

Psalm 104:33

The other day here at the College of Biblical Studies, we had a student group lead our faculty and staff chapel in music, worship, and prayer before the Lord.

There is something profoundly refreshing in singing your prayers to God. Psalm 104:33 says, "I will sing to the Lord as long as I live. I will sing praise to my God while I have my being."

If it's been a while since you lifted your voice in song to God, here is a word to the wise.

Don't let self-consciousness hold you back. Take some time to contemplate who Christ is and what He's done for you. Then let it out. Sing to Him with all your heart!

Today I will apply this wisdom in my life in the following ways:

_____

_____

To listen to this
Word to the Wise,
use your smart device
to scan the QR code!

June 2

Bacon's Ready!

I Corinthians 13:4

Dr. Evans said, "A woman does not marry a paycheck. She marries a man. She wants her husband's love, attention – and not just his business card."

In I Corinthians 13:4, it says that "love is kind." While patience describes that one is slow to anger, kindness emphasizes that someone is quick to serve, love, and care for one another. How kind are you to your spouse?

If this is an area that needs improvement, here is a word to the wise.

Marriage is made up of many kind and loving moments, so while it's okay to bring home the bacon, it's even better to **cook** it and **serve** it once in a while.

Today I will apply this wisdom in my life in the following ways:

_____

_____

To listen to this
Word to the Wise,
use your smart device
to scan the QR code!

June 3

Live and Let Live

Romans 15:7

Jerry Bridges said, "All too often we think we're standing on principle when in reality we may only be insisting on our opinion."

Some in the early church were convinced that their personal convictions were godlier than others' in the church. Neither conviction was necessarily sinful in and of itself, but the differing opinions were causing a rift. Paul wrote in Romans 15:7, "Accept one another just as Christ also accepted us to the glory of God."

If you and your preferences are causing friction in your relationships, here is a word to the wise.

Live for the Lord and let others live for the Lord. And remember: **you're not the Lord**.

Today I will apply this wisdom in my life in the following ways:

_____

_____

To listen to this
Word to the Wise,
use your smart device
to scan the QR code!

June 4

A Time to Hate

Luke 14:26

Some people might think that Christians should never hate, but according to Jesus, that's not always the case.

In Luke 14:26, He states, "If anyone comes to Me and does not hate his own mother and father and wife and children and brothers and sisters, yes, and even his own life, he cannot be My disciple." So, what does this mean?

Here is a word to the wise.

Anything or anyone who has higher priority in our lives than Jesus must be rejected as supreme and be brought back into its proper place. So, if hate means to love less, it's okay when you desire to **love Jesus <u>the most</u>**.

Today I will apply this wisdom in my life in the following ways:

_____

_____

To listen to this
Word to the Wise,
use your smart device
to scan the QR code!

June 5

Guard Your Mind

Proverbs 4:23

A Roman poet once said, "Rule your mind or it will rule you."

God's Word confirms this to be true. In Proverbs 4:23, we read, "More than all that you guard, guard your mind, for it is the source of life."

What do you think about the most? Here is a word to the wise.

Be careful. What you fill your mind with will ultimately influence how you live, what you say, and even the entire direction of your life. Take time to focus on God and His Word. It will truly keep your mind in perfect peace and your life will produce eternal treasures in heaven.

Today I will apply this wisdom in my life in the following ways:

_____

_____

To listen to this
Word to the Wise,
use your smart device
to scan the QR code!

June 6

I Will Not Be Afraid

Psalm 56:8

Do you ever feel like life has you on the run?

David felt that way when he was fleeing from Saul. In Psalm 56:8, David prayed, "You have taken account of my wanderings; put my tears in Your bottle. Are they not in Your book?" David had God's promise that he would be king, but he felt like a fugitive.

If you are not sure if you are heading in the right direction or just running from one difficulty to the next, here is a word to the wise.

God knows where you've been and where you are going. So, cry out with David, "In God have I put my trust. I will not be afraid."

Today I will apply this wisdom in my life in the following ways:

_____

_____

To listen to this
Word to the Wise,
use your smart device
to scan the QR code!

June 7

More Grace, Please

James 4:6

Did you know that God gives more grace to some than others? How can this be since grace is unmerited favor?

In James 4:6, he says a humble person receives a greater grace because "God is opposed to the proud, but He gives grace to the humble." Why? A proud person doesn't think he needs God's grace.

Do you think you need more grace? If so, here is a word to the wise.

God knows your situation and is always near. Ask God to search your heart for any signs of pride and remove it. By doing this, you'll experience that God's amazing grace is always sufficient.

Today I will apply this wisdom in my life in the following ways:

_____

_____

To listen to this
Word to the Wise,
use your smart device
to scan the QR code!

June 8

Plug In!

Romans 12:10

When you think of devotion, what comes to mind?

In Romans 12, the apostle Paul says that the mark of one who is being transformed by the gospel is devotion, in particular, devotion to other believers. He writes, "Be devoted to one another in brotherly love. Give preference to one another in honor."

If you are devoted more to things than you are to people, here is a word to the wise.

God calls us to be devoted to one another, especially in the church. Pull the plug on your devotion to those electronic devices and entertainment – and plug in to God's people.

Today I will apply this wisdom in my life in the following ways:

_____

_____

To listen to this
Word to the Wise,
use your smart device
to scan the QR code!

June 9

Where Is Your Safe Haven?

Do you long for healthy relationships but don't know where to begin?

Has work become a war zone? Your marriage a shouting contest? Has your bathroom become your safe haven?

Here is a word to the wise.

There are bad habits that you will definitely want to avoid and good habits that you want to cultivate in your relationships. Jesus in the Gospels displayed these good habits. Jesus exchanged the bad for the good, bitterness for forgiveness, pain for healing, and unhappiness for joy.

If you long for healthy relationships, get out of the bathroom! Let the power of the gospel, which is the Word of God, become your safe haven.

Today I will apply this wisdom in my life in the following ways:

_____

_____

To listen to this
Word to the Wise,
use your smart device
to scan the QR code!

June 10

Pessimism to Praise

Proverbs 17:20

Have you ever heard the saying, "I'm not pessimistic, just stating the facts"?

All of us can sometimes fall into a pattern of cynicism.

If you've ever felt your spirit descending into a cloud of negativity, suspicion, and criticism, here is a word to the wise.

Proverbs 17:20 tells us, "He who has a crooked mind finds no good, and he who is perverted in his language falls into evil." Train yourself to think biblically. Straight thinking based on the Word of God will produce purified lips. The real fact is, when we think realistically about God's grace toward us, our *pessimism* will give way to **praise**.

Today I will apply this wisdom in my life in the following ways:

_____

_____

To listen to this
Word to the Wise,
use your smart device
to scan the QR code!

June 11

Religion and Relationship

James 1:27

What type of religious activity does God desire?

Is it money, church attendance, or Bible memorization? His answer may surprise you.

In James 1:27, it says, "Pure and undefiled religion in the sight of our God and Father is this, to visit orphans and widows in their distress and to keep oneself unstained by the world." Surprising?

Here is a word to the wise.

People say that Christianity is not a religion but a relationship. James says it's both. Christianity is a religion that requires a relationship with God and those whom He cares most about.

Today I will apply this wisdom in my life in the following ways:

_____

_____

To listen to this
Word to the Wise,
use your smart device
to scan the QR code!

No Peace?

Psalm 3:4-6

Charles Spurgeon said, "All of our perils are as nothing so long as we have prayer."

Psalm 3 says that David prayed about his enemies, then went to sleep and awoke safe and sound because the Lord sustained him. He declared, "I will not be afraid of ten thousands of people who have set themselves against me."

If you've ever prayed about an issue only to find yourself worrying about it immediately after you said "amen," here is a word to the wise.

If you try to keep a piece of your problem to handle yourself, you will have no real peace. Entrust yourself and your circumstances wholly to Jesus — and then rest.

Today I will apply this wisdom in my life in the following ways:

_____

_____

To listen to this
Word to the Wise,
use your smart device
to scan the QR code!

June 13

Love Is the Answer

John 13:35

Sometimes it can feel difficult to share your faith with others.

Should it be the mail carrier? The cashier at the grocery store? Your boss? What would you say? How do people even know that you're following Christ?

Evangelism, good works, and your relationship with Christ are great ways for others to know, but John 13:35 says, "By this all people will know that you are My disciples, if you have love one for another."

Here is a word to the wise.

Demonstrate your faithfulness to Christ through love wherever you are — at home, at work, with friends and family, and even strangers — and they will surely see the Christ in you.

Today I will apply this wisdom in my life in the following ways:

_____

_____

To listen to this
Word to the Wise,
use your smart device
to scan the QR code!

June 14

Ready for Battle?

Ephesians 6:18

It has been said, "A prayerless man is a careless man."

In Ephesians 6, the apostle Paul wrote, "With all prayer and petition, pray at all times in the Spirit." He understood that a soldier may have all of his equipment, but his dependence on God is the one element that makes the armor effective.

If you have been careless in approaching your spiritual battles, here is a word to the wise.

Prayer in keeping with God's Word, in the Spirit, is the key to the armor's proper use. If you want to ultimately win the day, put on your armor, and consistently look to God and pray.

Today I will apply this wisdom in my life in the following ways:

_____

_____

To listen to this
Word to the Wise,
use your smart device
to scan the QR code!

June 15

Matthew 5 Special
Matthew 5:6

Have you ever gone to a fancy restaurant to eat and felt hungry one hour later?

Charles Spurgeon said, "When Jesus is the host, no guest goes empty from the table."

So, how is it that many hear the Word of God and are still empty? The answer may be found in Matthew 5:6. It says, "Blessed are those who hunger and thirst for righteousness for they shall be satisfied."

Do you hunger and thirst for righteousness like you do food? Here is a word to the wise.

As you approach God's Word, come hungry for what I call the "Matthew 5 Special" and you will find satisfaction for your soul!

Today I will apply this wisdom in my life in the following ways:

_____

_____

To listen to this *Word to the Wise*, use your smart device to scan the QR code!

June 16

Well Done

Colossians 3:23

One of my first paying jobs was working in a drive-through at McDonald's.

One Friday during rush hour, the demand for cheeseburgers overwhelmed Sarah, our grill lady, so much that she started sending up half-done quarter pounders. Needless to say, Sarah was fired. Unfortunately, we as Christians try to cut corners in the same manner when we're overcome with difficulties or become frustrated.

If you're guilty of rendering half-done services, here is a word to the wise.

Paul says in Colossians 3:23, "And whatsoever you do, do it heartily as unto the Lord and not unto men." Why? Because in the end we want to hear God say, <u>not half</u>, but **well done**!

Today I will apply this wisdom in my life in the following ways:

_____

_____

To listen to this
Word to the Wise,
use your smart device
to scan the QR code!

June 17

Inside Out

I Samuel 16

Have you heard the saying, "Don't judge a book by its cover"?

In I Samuel 16, Samuel was certain that the oldest son of Jesse was of royal material. He was tall and handsome, but God selected David and corrected Samuel. How? By confirming that He looks not on the outside but on the inside.

If you are guilty of prejudging by outward appearances, here is a word to the wise.

God judges the heart and not the face. While you may be looking at others from the *outside*, please remember that God is looking at us on the *inside*.

Today I will apply this wisdom in my life in the following ways:

_____

_____

To listen to this
Word to the Wise,
use your smart device
to scan the QR code!

June 18

Be Your Own Fire Extinguisher

Proverbs 16:27

Before 9/11, Americans could hardly fathom the evil that took place.

There are people in this world that only seek to destroy and tear us down.

Did you know that the tongue has the same power? Proverbs 16:27 says, "A worthless man plots evil and his speech is like a scorching fire."

Do you have a problem with your tongue? Are you constantly being reminded to think before you speak? Here is a word to the wise.

Ask God to season your speech with love, or **you** may be setting **your** own house on fire!

Today I will apply this wisdom in my life in the following ways:

_____

_____

To listen to this
Word to the Wise,
use your smart device
to scan the QR code!

June 19

He's Got This

II Peter 2:9

Throughout the ages many people have asked why God allows evil to exist.

Many get stuck on the question of evil, especially when we suffer unjustly. How can we surrender our lives to a God who is either ambivalent to cruelty or powerless to do anything about it?

Look throughout Scripture and find hope. Evil does not win in the end. God said, "Vengeance is mine; I shall repay."

If evil is pressing you down, here is a word to the wise.

In II Peter 2:9, he says, "The Lord knows how to rescue godly men from trials and to hold the unrighteous for the Day of Judgment."

Today I will apply this wisdom in my life in the following ways:

_____

_____

To listen to this *Word to the Wise,* use your smart device to scan the QR code!

June 20

Divine Satisfaction

Mark 7:24-30

How do you respond when God's answers to your petitions aren't exactly what you expected?

A woman once asked Jesus for help, to which He said, "It's not good to take the children's bread and throw it to dogs." Instead of taking offense, she said, "Lord, but even the dogs under the table feed on the children's crumbs." Jesus granted the woman her request.

Are you easily offended in your faith? Here is a word to the wise.

Don't let your pride keep you from receiving your answer. A plate full of pride is empty, but even the crumbs of divine grace satisfy.

Today I will apply this wisdom in my life in the following ways:

_____

_____

To listen to this
Word to the Wise,
use your smart device
to scan the QR code!

June 21

Rainbows

Genesis 9:11-16

When you see a rainbow, what do you think of?

Some may think of a mythical pot of gold at its end; others may equate it with some social or cultural movement. But according to Genesis 9, the rainbow was given after the judgment of Noah's flood as an ongoing reminder of God's faithfulness and mercy in regard to His creation.

If you're more prone to think of leprechauns and legends or pride and promiscuity, here is a word to the wise.

The rainbow is a sign of divine patience and unfailing faithfulness. The next time you see a rainbow, remember the judgment of the flood – and praise God for His tender mercies to sinners who trust in Christ!

Today I will apply this wisdom in my life in the following ways:

_____

_____

To listen to this
Word to the Wise,
use your smart device
to scan the QR code!

Go Ahead, Make My Day!

James 2:1-13

Clint Eastwood said, "The less secure a man is, the more likely he is to have extreme prejudice."

The Bible in James 2 calls believers to embrace all men alike without partiality. It says that prejudice is a violation of God's law on par with murder and adultery.

If you find it difficult to reach out to those who are different from you, here is a word to the wise.

Jesus set aside His privileged position to reach out to you in love. Your identity is secure in Christ. So, go ahead, make my day! Open your hand and your heart to others because **mercy** triumphs over judgment.

Today I will apply this wisdom in my life in the following ways:

_____

_____

To listen to this
Word to the Wise,
use your smart device
to scan the QR code!

June 23

Illusion of Control

Psalm 90:12

Our culture often tells us that we must always be in control. "Don't let anyone run your life."

However, this really is an illusion. If we could control our lives, we would determine how long we lived on the earth. In Psalm 90:12, it says, "Teach us to number our days that we may gain the heart of wisdom."

If you are struggling with control issues, here is a word to the wise.

Pray today that the Lord will examine your heart. Then surrender everything to the Lord. Only when you are willing to release your priorities and the illusion of control to the will of the Lord, will you discover true freedom.

Today I will apply this wisdom in my life in the following ways:

_____

_____

To listen to this
Word to the Wise,
use your smart device
to scan the QR code!

June 24

Cooked Goose for Dinner

James 1:19-21

It's been said, "Nothing can cook your goose quicker than boiling anger."

James 1:19 says, "This you know, my beloved brethren, but everyone must be quick to hear, slow to speak, and slow to anger, for the anger of man does not achieve the righteousness of God."

If you feel your feathers getting ruffled a bit too often, here is a word to the wise.

James says, "In humility, receive the Word implanted, which is able to save your souls, but prove yourselves doers of the Word and not merely hearers." Let the Word of God cool your spirit, or else your anger will cook your goose!

Today I will apply this wisdom in my life in the following ways:

_____

_____

To listen to this
Word to the Wise,
use your smart device
to scan the QR code!

June 25

An Eternal "Thank You"

Galatians 6:9

Do you ever get tired of feeling overlooked and underappreciated in your efforts to bless others?

In Galatians 6:9, the apostle Paul encourages believers who are sowing for a spiritual harvest. "Let us not lose heart in doing good, for in due time we will reap if we do not grow weary."

If this thankless world has left you feeling weary or weak in heart, here is a word to the wise.

Remember that you're not serving for the praise of men but rather for the pleasure and commendation of God. Don't get discouraged. Keep your eyes on the prize. Jesus is the One you serve, and His "Well done, My good and faithful servant," will be for eternity.

Today I will apply this wisdom in my life in the following ways:

_____

_____

To listen to this
Word to the Wise,
use your smart device
to scan the QR code!

June 26

Hedge or Highway?

Proverbs 15:19

John C. Maxwell said, "Hard work is the accumulation of easy things you didn't do when you should have."

Are you a procrastinator? Proverbs 15:19 says, "The way of the lazy is as a hedge of thorns, but the path of the upright is a highway."

If you are stuck in the thorns, here is a word to the wise.

Sometimes we postpone tasks because we're looking for a better time to do them; however, doing so only multiplies the problems rather than reducing them. Create a plan that works and then work your plan, and truly, you can find your rest.

Today I will apply this wisdom in my life in the following ways:

_____

_____

To listen to this
Word to the Wise,
use your smart device
to scan the QR code!

June 27

Now or Later?

John 18:37

Jesus said to Pilate in John 18:37, "For this I have come into the world, to testify to the truth. Everyone who is of the truth hears My voice," to which Pilate replied, "What is truth?"

Christ is *the* source of truth, but Pilate's life was based on political expediency.

If you are having trouble distinguishing truth from error, here is a word to the wise.

Each day we are faced with a decision: Listen to the voice of self-interest or listen to the voice of Christ the King. Self-interest may preserve your position for the moment, but listening to the voice of Jesus will preserve your place in eternity.

Today I will apply this wisdom in my life in the following ways:

_____

_____

To listen to this
Word to the Wise,
use your smart device
to scan the QR code!

June 28

Don't Go Back

Romans 6:21

Ben Franklin once said, "Sin is not hurtful because it's forbidden but forbidden because it is hurtful."

Did you know that when you sin it not only hurts you but also those who are closest to you? Romans 6:21 says, "Therefore what benefit were you then deriving from the things of which you are now ashamed? For the outcome of those things is death."

If you are struggling with the impact of your sin, here is a word to the wise.

God has freed you from the snares of death caused by sin. If God has set you free, stop going back to the hurtful bonds of sin!

Today I will apply this wisdom in my life in the following ways:

_____

_____

To listen to this
Word to the Wise,
use your smart device
to scan the QR code!

June 29

To Fear or Not to Fear?

Exodus 20:20

Dr. Tom Constable wrote, "The fear of the Lord includes a desire not to sin against Him because His wrath is so awful and His love is so awesome."

In Exodus 20:20, Moses told Israel, "Do not be afraid for God has come in order to test you and in order that the fear of Him may remain with you." So, which is it, fear or no fear?

Here is a word to the wise.

There is a difference between hellish fear and healthy fear. One brings torment; the other is tonic to our soul. Jesus bore the awful wrath so that we might know His awesome love. It's okay! Don't be afraid to fear God.

Today I will apply this wisdom in my life in the following ways:

_____

_____

To listen to this
Word to the Wise,
use your smart device
to scan the QR code!

June 30

Substituting Service for Solidarity

Luke 10:41-42

We are all probably familiar with the story of Mary and Martha.

I'm reminded of what Jesus said to Martha. "Martha, Martha, you are worried and bothered about so many things, but only one thing is necessary. Mary has chosen the good part, which shall not be taken away from her."

Are you guilty of substituting your service for solidarity with Christ?

If your service is distracting you from your communion with the Lord, here is a word to the wise.

Ask God to help you prioritize and refocus your intimate time with Christ. Sitting at the Master's feet is the one thing that's absolutely necessary.

Today I will apply this wisdom in my life in the following ways:

_____

_____

To listen to this
Word to the Wise,
use your smart device
to scan the QR code!

July 1

Don't Worry About Tomorrow

Matthew 6:25-34

Corrie Ten Boom said, "Worry does not empty tomorrow of its sorrow. It empties today of its strength."

Do you wrestle with worry? Jesus gave an antidote for worry in Matthew 6:33, when He says, "Seek first God's kingdom and His righteousness." He did not say, however, don't *think* about tomorrow, but rather do not worry about it.

If your worrying is weighing you down, here is a word to the wise.

Rather than focusing on the things you cannot change, start pursuing the things that God says are righteous. Then say goodbye to your worrying and you will find strength for your journey.

Today I will apply this wisdom in my life in the following ways:

_____

_____

To listen to this
Word to the Wise,
use your smart device
to scan the QR code!

July 2

Sold Out for Jesus

Mark 5

How you respond to Jesus is more of a commentary on who *you* are than who *He* is.

In Mark 5, there are three different types of responses to Jesus as He healed the demoniac. The demons were *terrified* of Jesus, the owners of the pigs were *troubled* by Jesus, but the man that was delivered was *thirsty* for Jesus, begging to follow Him wherever He went.

If you're terrified and troubled about your response to Christ, here is a word to the wise.

Make following Christ your number one priority. This is the only correct response, and your commentary will read, "Sold out for Jesus!"

Today I will apply this wisdom in my life in the following ways:

_____

_____

To listen to this
Word to the Wise,
use your smart device
to scan the QR code!

July 3

How to Escape Sin's Deathtrap

Romans 6:18

George MacDonald said, "In short, a man must be set free from the sin he is, which makes him do the sin he does."

Did you know that any effort we do to fix our own sin makes it muddy? It's like trying to keep a pig who loves mud, clean.

If you want to be free from the stain of sin, here is a word to the wise.

Romans 6:18 says, "You have been set free from sin and have become slaves to righteousness." Without Christ, every man and woman lives in the depravity of sin. There's only one solution for sin's deathtrap. Accept Jesus Christ today and be free.

Today I will apply this wisdom in my life in the following ways:

_____

_____

To listen to this *Word to the Wise,* use your smart device to scan the QR code!

July 4

License to Carry

Ephesians 6:17

Did you know that God wants all Christians to be armed and dangerous?

In Ephesians 6:17, the apostle Paul calls us to take the "sword of the Spirit, which is the Word of God." The sword spoken of here was a dagger-like weapon used for hand-to-hand combat. It was both precise and deadly.

If you're feeling vulnerable to the attacks of the adversary, here is a word to the wise.

When the enemy assails us, we need to know how to skillfully apply the Word of God to each temptation. So, arm yourselves with the Scriptures. God gives you the license to carry!

Today I will apply this wisdom in my life in the following ways:

_____

_____

To listen to this
Word to the Wise,
use your smart device
to scan the QR code!

July 5

Sooner Than Later

Isaiah 55:7

Isaac Barrow once said, "Sin is never at a stay. If we do not retreat from it, we shall advance in it, and the farther we go, the more we have to come back."

Yes, it is true that God welcomes us back with abundant forgiveness when we repent; however, we can save ourselves a great deal of pain by returning sooner than later.

Have you sunk too far in sin? Here is a word to the wise.

Isaiah 55:7 says, "Let the wicked forsake his way and the unrighteous man his thoughts, and let him return to the Lord and He will have compassion on him." Come home today. God is waiting!

Today I will apply this wisdom in my life in the following ways:

_____

_____

To listen to this *Word to the Wise,* use your smart device to scan the QR code!

July 6

Freedom in the Sovereignty of God

Psalm 115:3

Many of us have said God is sovereign, but do we really know what that means?

"Sovereignty" means supreme power, ultimate control, and the authority to rule — freedom from external control. Psalm 115:3 says, "Our God is in the heavens. He does whatever He pleases."

If you've never grasped the freedom that comes from resting in the sovereignty of God, here is a word to the wise.

Since He is infinitely good and all powerful, He always does what is good in every situation. Even when our circumstances look bleak, <u>trust in God's sovereign wisdom</u> and remember to wait for His sovereign blessing.

Today I will apply this wisdom in my life in the following ways:

_____

_____

To listen to this
Word to the Wise,
use your smart device
to scan the QR code!

July 7

Praise You, Jesus!

Proverbs 11:2

Charles Spurgeon once said, "The more thou hast, the more thou art in debt to God and the more thou shouldest not be proud of that which renders thee a debtor."

The Bible says in Proverbs 11, "When pride comes, then comes dishonor, but with the humble is wisdom." Pride is an ugly, dishonorable thing because it grants credit to oneself for something that only God should receive.

Are you filled with pride but would like to have wisdom? Here is a word to the wise.

A wise person realizes that everything he has is the result of the grace of God. So, give praise to God instead of seeking praise for yourself!

Today I will apply this wisdom in my life in the following ways:

_____

_____

To listen to this
Word to the Wise,
use your smart device
to scan the QR code!

July 8

Boast in the Lord

I Corinthians 1:30

We live in a culture that defines worth by physical attractiveness, our earning power, and the success of our families.

These false worldly standards create dangerous disunity among Christians as they did during the apostle Paul's day. Paul points to the real benchmark in I Corinthians 1:30 when he says that we have the standard of Christ crucified, the wisdom of God who is our "righteousness, holiness, and redemption."

Are you being deceived by worldly standards? Here is a word to the wise.

The most important thing we possess in life comes from the Lord. As it is written, "Let him who boasts, boast in the Lord."

Today I will apply this wisdom in my life in the following ways:

_____

_____

To listen to this
Word to the Wise,
use your smart device
to scan the QR code!

July 9

Joy in the Midst of Suffering

Job 42:1-6

It has been said, "Joy is not necessarily the absence of suffering; it is the presence of God."

Job suffered beyond what most of us can imagine, but when God revealed His power and wisdom to Job, he found consolation even though still afflicted.

Are you currently suffering or experiencing difficulty? Here is a word to the wise.

Remember that both Job and the apostle Paul learned about weakness, suffering, and difficulty. God's grace is sufficient for you, and His power is perfected in your weakness. So, while suffering is sometimes unavoidable, have joy in knowing that our all-powerful God is always present with you.

Today I will apply this wisdom in my life in the following ways:

_____

_____

To listen to this
Word to the Wise,
use your smart device
to scan the QR code!

July 10

Please Stand Up

Isaiah 1:17

Benjamin Franklin said, "Justice will not be served until those who are unaffected are as outraged as those who are."

It is one thing to be concerned for the poor and those who are hurting, but does your compassion enflame you into action? Isaiah 1:17 says, "Learn to do good, seek justice, reprove the ruthless, defend the orphan, and plead for the widow."

To those who want to make a difference, here is a word to the wise.

Take a biblical stand. The God who justifies sinners and brings justice to the hurting will also give you the strength, knowledge, and passion to do so.

Today I will apply this wisdom in my life in the following ways:

_____

_____

To listen to this
Word to the Wise,
use your smart device
to scan the QR code!

July 11

All Your Heart

Proverbs 21:3

Augustine said, "Don't let your life give evidence against your tongue. Sing with your voices. Sing also with your conduct."

No doubt God calls us to praise Him with our lips, but He also calls us to praise Him with our lives. Proverbs 21:3 says, "To do what is right and true is more pleasing to the Lord than an offering."

If you find it easier to sing hymns of praise than to submit to His precepts, here is a word to the wise.

Don't compartmentalize your worship. Sing with all your might and seek to obey God's Word with all your heart!

Today I will apply this wisdom in my life in the following ways:

_____

_____

To listen to this
Word to the Wise,
use your smart device
to scan the QR code!

July 12

Looking for a Few Good Men and Women

I Corinthians 1:27

Dr. John Piper said, "The difference between Uncle Sam and Jesus Christ is that Uncle Sam won't enlist you in his service unless you're healthy, and Jesus won't enlist you unless you're sick."

This is good news, because many Christians today are struggling with God's calling on their lives: "I don't have any gifts. How can God use me?"

Do you feel that you're not good enough to be used by God? Here is a word to the wise.

In I Corinthians 1:27, it says, "God has chosen the foolish things of the world to shame the wise, and God has chosen the weak things of the world to shame the things which are strong." In other words, God is not looking for the wise, strong, and mighty, but faithful servants to enlist in His army. So what are you waiting for?

Today I will apply this wisdom in my life in the following ways:

_____

_____

To listen to this
Word to the Wise,
use your smart device
to scan the QR code!

July 13

The Cross Will Shield You

Ephesians 6:16

It's been said, "Faith is the capacity to trust God while not being able to make sense out of everything."

In Ephesians 6, the apostle Paul calls believers to take up the "shield of faith" which "extinguishes all the flaming arrows of the evil one."

If you've ever experienced the fiery darts of doubt and fear, here is a word to the wise.

When you feel like you are a target for the enemy, keep trusting God's Word. The adversary will soon run out of ammunition. No fear or demonic accusation can pierce the one who hides behind the power of the cross.

Today I will apply this wisdom in my life in the following ways:

_____

_____

To listen to this
Word to the Wise,
use your smart device
to scan the QR code!

July 14

Where Is *Your* Focus?

Hebrews 12:2

Charles Spurgeon said, "It is ever the Holy Spirit's work to turn our eyes away from self and to Jesus; but Satan's work is just the opposite, for he is constantly trying to make us regard ourselves instead of Christ."

Where is your focus? Hebrews 12:2 commands us to fix our eyes on Jesus, the author and perfecter of our faith.

For those of you who want to keep your eyes on Jesus, here is a word to the wise.

Jesus endured the cross because He did not focus on Himself. Make the right choice. Look at self and be discouraged, or turn to Christ and be delivered.

Today I will apply this wisdom in my life in the following ways:

_____

_____

To listen to this
Word to the Wise,
use your smart device
to scan the QR code!

Are You Really There, God?

Genesis 15:6

Would a person of true faith ever question God?

Abram did in Genesis 15; yet, it says, "Abram believed the Lord and the Lord counted him as righteous because of his faith." There is a difference between faithless challenges and the genuine questions of one who trusts the Lord.

If you're wondering if God is listening, here is a word to the wise.

An embittered demand will fall on deaf ears, but a submissive challenge to fulfill His Word, God will always hear. Go ahead, bring your questions to the Lord. But you must remember to have a believing heart.

Today I will apply this wisdom in my life in the following ways:

_____

_____

To listen to this
Word to the Wise,
use your smart device
to scan the QR code!

July 16

It Don't Come Easy — But It's Worth the *Weight*

II Corinthians 4:17

Paul David Tripp said, "If God intended for every day of your life to be easy, it would be, but in grace and love He permits difficult days to refine you."

Are you primarily looking for a life of ease or holiness? Second Corinthians 4:17 says, "For this *light* momentary affliction is preparing for us an eternal *weight* of glory beyond all comparison."

For those of you who are suffering, here is a word to the wise.

Yes, all Christians face trials and hardships of various kinds. While you may not understand the reason for the suffering in this life, He is making you holy so that you can fully appreciate all He has for you in eternity.

Today I will apply this wisdom in my life in the following ways:

_____

_____

To listen to this
Word to the Wise,
use your smart device
to scan the QR code!

198

July 17

Love Divine
Genesis 1:31

Have you ever questioned why the world is the way it is?

In Genesis 1:31, it says that after God was done with the original creation, He "saw all that He had made and, behold, it was very good." But today, the world is not very good. There is injustice, hatred, pain, and death. Why? Man's sin. Genesis tells us that man chose to rebel against his Creator and disobey His Word.

Here is a word to the wise.

There is hope. God promises deliverance from sin to those who turn to Christ in faith. So, why would God send His Son to save rebellious sinners? Why? **Divine love.**

Today I will apply this wisdom in my life in the following ways:

_____

_____

To listen to this
Word to the Wise,
use your smart device
to scan the QR code!

July 18

God's GPS

Proverbs 11:3

E. M. Bounds said, "The church is looking for better methods. God is looking for better men."

As a Christian, how is your integrity?

Proverbs 11:3 says, "The integrity of the upright will guide them, but the crookedness of the treacherous will destroy them."

Here is a word to the wise.

The biblical notion of integrity is to be complete in purity and character. This integrity is like a GPS that guides the believer even through the most difficult of situations. So, ditch those self-help books and allow the power of God's Word to make you a better man or woman!

Today I will apply this wisdom in my life in the following ways:

_____

_____

To listen to this
Word to the Wise,
use your smart device
to scan the QR code!

July 19

Abba and *Adonai*

Psalm 89:6-7

If you or I had an audience before the Chief Justice of the Supreme Court, we would likely be a little bit in awe of the privilege we had to express our concerns before a person of such high position.

But have you ever considered the privilege we have in prayer? Psalm 89:6-7 says, "Who in the skies is comparable to the Lord, a God greatly feared in the counsel of the holy ones and awesome above those who are all around Him?"

If you've ever taken prayer for granted, here is a word to the wise.

The God we call Father is the God before whom angels bow in reverence. When you pray, remember, our gracious *Abba* is also our glorious *Adonai*.

Today I will apply this wisdom in my life in the following ways:

_____

_____

To listen to this *Word to the Wise*, use your smart device to scan the QR code!

July 20

Life of Greatness

Ecclesiastes 12

I saw a bumper sticker that read, "I live for golf."

What are you actually living for? What you are living for is evident not by some statement you have hanging around your house or even on your car, but what you actually do, pursue, and embrace.

Many times we allow what is good to rob us of what is great. Here is a word to the wise.

Live for what matters most. Don't allow what is good to keep you from focusing on what is great. Yes, work hard, but don't live for work. Have fun, but don't live for amusement. Learn from Solomon who said in Ecclesiastes 12, if you live for God, then your life will count for something great!

Today I will apply this wisdom in my life in the following ways:

_____

_____

To listen to this
Word to the Wise,
use your smart device
to scan the QR code!

July 21

Stop Stoking the Fire!

Proverbs 26:20-21

Troublemakers – we all know them and we all dislike them.

Leave it to a troublemaker to make a bad situation worse.

How can you tell? Proverbs 26:21 says, "As charcoal is to hot embers and wood to fire, so is a quarrelsome man for kindling strife."

Here is a word to the wise.

If you find yourself in a quarreling situation, take a note from Proverbs 26:20 where it says, "For lack of wood, the fire goes out, and where there is no whisperer, quarreling ceases." In other words, stop adding wood to the fire!

Today I will apply this wisdom in my life in the following ways:

_____

_____

To listen to this
Word to the Wise,
use your smart device
to scan the QR code!

July 22

Almost Right

Hebrews 5:14

Charles Spurgeon said, "Discernment is not a matter of simply telling the difference between right and wrong. Rather, it is telling the difference between right and almost right."

Only constant interaction with the Word of God, and its proper interpretation and application, develops the ability to distinguish truth from error. Hebrews 5:14 tells us that a lifelong pursuit of studying the Scripture trains a believer to discern good and evil.

If you are in need of greater discernment, here is a word to the wise.

Almost right is still wrong. So, develop **your** discernment today – keep studying the Scriptures.

Today I will apply this wisdom in my life in the following ways:

_____

_____

To listen to this
Word to the Wise,
use your smart device
to scan the QR code!

July 23

Everywhere and Always There

Matthew 28:20

Many nonbelievers picture God as far away.

Sometimes, as Christians, there are times in our lives when we feel that God is at a distance and is not present specifically in our trials.

Have you ever felt like this? When you needed God most, He was absent? God's omnipresence not only assures us that God is *everywhere*, but affirms that God is *always* there.

If you are questioning God's whereabouts, here is a word to the wise.

As you go through difficult times in your life, take comfort in Christ's words in Matthew 28:20 where He says, "Lo, I am with you always, even to the end of the age."

Today I will apply this wisdom in my life in the following ways:

_____

_____

To listen to this
Word to the Wise,
use your smart device
to scan the QR code!

July 24

Compassionate Holiness

Mark 1:40-41

In all of history, who alone lived a sinless and perfectly holy life?

Jesus, of course, but His holiness did not compel Him to avoid people. Rather, it seemed to have prompted Him to help them. There are at least eight references in the Gospel accounts of Jesus feeling or having compassion on people. He was moved emotionally and physically to care for those who were lost and in need.

If you've never thought about the connection between holiness and compassion, here is a word to the wise.

If you want to truly be holy, stay away from sin, but don't be afraid of loving sinners. If that's a challenge, remember, Jesus loves *you*.

Today I will apply this wisdom in my life in the following ways:

_____

_____

To listen to this
Word to the Wise,
use your smart device
to scan the QR code!

July 25

Celebrating Diversity

Revelation 7:9

The other day someone asked me why I came to the College of Biblical Studies.

My answer came almost without thinking. Most other Bible colleges are training people to go out and minister to a diverse world, but at the College of Biblical Studies, *we are the diverse world*. Have you ever considered the diversity of people, cultures, and languages around you?

Here is a word to the wise.

Revelation 7:9 reminds us that heaven will be filled with a great multitude from every nation and culture on earth. So, the next time you're in the company of people that seem very different from you, relax! Let it be a reminder to celebrate the grace of God in Jesus Christ.

Today I will apply this wisdom in my life in the following ways:

_____

_____

To listen to this *Word to the Wise,* use your smart device to scan the QR code!

July 26

Joy to the World!

Philippians 4:4

Have you ever been to a place where the people are in a bad mood? How does that influence your perception of that place?

Dr. John Piper once said, "God is most glorified when we are most satisfied in Him." Philippians 4:4 says, "Rejoice in the Lord always. Again, I will say, rejoice."

If your attitude is sending the wrong message, here is a word to the wise.

Christians are God's marketing plan to the world of the joy that is found in the worship of His Son, Jesus. We have the most reason to be joyful, and the world should notice our joy!

Today I will apply this wisdom in my life in the following ways:

_____

_____

To listen to this
Word to the Wise,
use your smart device
to scan the QR code!

July 27

What's Your Name?

Proverbs 22:1; Micah 6:8

Did you know your name has value?

According to Proverbs 22:1, it says, "A good name is more desirable than great riches." The value of your name, however, is in direct proportion to your character. If you mention a name, people will remember something about that person's character.

If you desire to keep your good name, here is a word to the wise.

Micah 6:8 calls believers to seek justice, love mercy, and walk humbly before God. Make a commitment to do God's will. May it be that whenever your name is mentioned, people smile and thank God for the **Christ in you**!

Today I will apply this wisdom in my life in the following ways:

_____

_____

To listen to this
Word to the Wise,
use your smart device
to scan the QR code!

July 28

Divine Appointments

James 4:13-15

Have you ever watched your breath disappear on a cold morning?

James 4 says that life is like a "vapor that appears for a little while and then vanishes away."

If you're wondering how to live life in light of life's rapidly changing circumstances, here is a word to the wise.

God calls us to make our plans with Him in mind. James continues by saying, "If the Lord wills, we will also do this or that." God isn't asking for magic words, but rather an attitude of submission to His sovereign will. So plan your tomorrow in pencil – and leave room for divine appointments.

Today I will apply this wisdom in my life in the following ways:

_____

_____

To listen to this
Word to the Wise,
use your smart device
to scan the QR code!

Thank Him for Unanswered Prayer

II Corinthians 12:9

Can you imagine what life would be like if God answered all of our prayers?

You would be married to a short-lived crush, doing the same job that you no longer like, and having stuff that you can't stand. Fortunately, God does not graciously give us everything we want.

Once, God chose not to answer the apostle Paul's prayers and He said to him in II Corinthians 12:9, "My grace is sufficient for you, for power is perfected in weakness."

If you're struggling with God answering your prayers, here is a word to the wise.

In addition to thanking God for the prayers He did answer, take some time to thank Him for the prayers He **didn't** answer!

Today I will apply this wisdom in my life in the following ways:

_____

_____

To listen to this
Word to the Wise,
use your smart device
to scan the QR code!

July 30

Wait for It ...

James 5:7-11

To paraphrase Jerry Bridges, "Patience is the ability to suffer a long time under difficulty without growing resentful or bitter." But how long is long enough?

God calls us to wait for the Lord's coming like a farmer for the harvest. And while we wait, let's remember the outcome of God's dealing with Job: The Lord is full of compassion and merciful.

If you're finding yourself short on patience, here is a word to the wise.

James 5 says, "Be patient, brethren, until the coming of the Lord." So, instead of giving up, keep looking up. Your Deliverer is coming!

Today I will apply this wisdom in my life in the following ways:

_____

_____

To listen to this
Word to the Wise,
use your smart device
to scan the QR code!

212

July 31

God's Grace Really Is Sufficient

II Corinthians 12

A few years back, I fell and dislocated my arm while playing basketball and it seemed like the pain would never, ever go away.

While pain is something very few like to experience, we as Christians are not exempt.

So, here's a question for you. How do you handle your pain? Do you become bitter, resentful, and angry? Take a note from the apostle Paul in II Corinthians 12 as he pleads to God three times to remove the painful thorn from his side. But God replies, "My grace is sufficient for you."

Here is a word to the wise.

If grace is enough to save you, surely it's enough to maintain you.

Today I will apply this wisdom in my life in the following ways:

_____

_____

To listen to this
Word to the Wise,
use your smart device
to scan the QR code!

August 1

World Peace

Genesis 11:1-9

What would life be like if the unbelieving world united with a common goal?

The Bible tells us about such a time. In Genesis 11, man united in opposition to God's Word and God's authority. The result is known as the Tower of Babel.

Is world unity really the answer to man's problems? Here is a word to the wise.

Only when Jesus returns to rule the earth will there be world unity that is genuinely beneficial to mankind. Until then, God has established nations and peoples and languages for the preservation of the world. So get ready for world peace and a unified humanity with *Jesus' return in glory*.

Today I will apply this wisdom in my life in the following ways:

_____

_____

To listen to this
Word to the Wise,
use your smart device
to scan the QR code!

August 2

Oh, My Aching Head!

Judges 18

The theme of our postmodern world could be summarized by Debbie Boone's old song, "You light up my life," as she sang, "It can't be wrong when it feels so right."

In Judges 18 the Danites picked the land by their sight instead of God's will. When they had seen the land, they said, "Behold, it is very good." But there was only one problem. God did not direct them to that land, and we can see in Jeremiah 8:15, all the invasions of Israel arrived in Dan first, and they were destroyed.

Are you struggling with your direction in life? Here is a word to the wise.

God's revealed Word is *always* best. When your feelings conflict with God's Word, <u>trust God's Word</u>. Trying to bypass God's plan will always cause greater headaches.

Today I will apply this wisdom in my life in the following ways:

_____

_____

To listen to this
Word to the Wise,
use your smart device
to scan the QR code!

August 3

Perfect Faithfulness

John 21

Albert Einstein once said, "A person who never made a mistake never tried anything new."

Peter experienced this firsthand when he denied Jesus three times.

If you've ever failed in living out your love for Christ, here is a word to the wise.

In John 21, even though Peter had failed Him three times, the resurrected Lord called Peter to serve Him and His people three times, matching his three denials. So the defining issue in life is not *our* perfect faithfulness in loving the Lord, but rather the *Lord's* perfect faithfulness in loving us. Now that's motivation to love and serve Christ, no matter your past failures!

Today I will apply this wisdom in my life in the following ways:

_____

_____

To listen to this
Word to the Wise,
use your smart device
to scan the QR code!

August 4

Never Shall You Wash My Feet

John 13:8

Have you ever noticed that sometimes, rather than letting Christ into the deepest, ugliest parts of our life, we prefer to try to clean them up on our own?

Unfortunately, when we do that, we don't embrace all the forgiveness that Christ has for us.

In John 13, Jesus tried to illustrate the importance of embracing His forgiveness by cleansing the disciples' feet. Peter said to Him, "Never shall You wash my feet," but Jesus answered and said, "If I don't wash your feet, you have no part with Me."

Are you like Peter? Here is a word to the wise.

Rather than trying to fix your past sins, will you embrace the fact that He has already washed you clean when you accepted Him?

Today I will apply this wisdom in my life in the following ways:

_____

_____

To listen to this
Word to the Wise,
use your smart device
to scan the QR code!

August 5

Remember Who You're Talking To

Ecclesiastes 5:2

John Bunyan said, "In prayer it's better to have a heart without words than words without a heart."

The psalmists make it clear that we can cry out to God in any and every circumstance, telling Him what's on our heart. But Ecclesiastes 5:2 warns us against thoughtless, inconsiderate prayer. It says, "Do not be hasty in word or impulsive in thought to bring a matter in the presence of God, for God is in heaven and you are on the earth; therefore, let your words be few."

If you've never considered the thoughtfulness of your prayers, here is a word to the wise.

Pray without ceasing. Just remember **who** you're talking to.

Today I will apply this wisdom in my life in the following ways:

_____

_____

To listen to this
Word to the Wise,
use your smart device
to scan the QR code!

August 6

Humbled yet Exalted

James 4:8-9

How can you approach God in humility?

The Bible tells us in James 4:8, "Draw near to God and He will draw near to you. Cleanse your hands, you sinners; and purify your hearts, you double-minded. Be miserable and mourn and weep and let your laughter be turned into mourning and your joy to gloom." When a humble person draws near to God, they are cleansing themselves of sin and from being double-minded.

As you look at your life, is there sin that you need to confess? Here is a word to the wise.

Is drawing near to God a priority in your life? Do you mourn over your sin? If not, humble yourself in the presence of God and He will in due time exalt **you**.

Today I will apply this wisdom in my life in the following ways:

_____

_____

To listen to this
Word to the Wise,
use your smart device
to scan the QR code!

August 7

Investing in the Future

I Timothy 6:17

John Wesley said, "I judge all things only by the price they shall gain in eternity." The money God gives us can bring both temporal and eternal rewards.

In I Timothy 6:17, Paul instructs those who are rich in the present world not to fix their hope on the uncertainty of riches, but rather on God.

If you want to accrue eternal dividends that will never decrease in a downturned market, here is a word to the wise.

Be generous and ready to share in God's economy. What are you waiting for? Invest in the glory of Christ and watch your eternal holdings rise.

Today I will apply this wisdom in my life in the following ways:

_____

_____

To listen to this
Word to the Wise,
use your smart device
to scan the QR code!

Shh ... I'm busy!

Nehemiah 6:3

Have you ever heard the saying, "A man who says it cannot be done should not interrupt the man who's doing it"?

Are you allowing your critics to keep you from doing God's work? In Nehemiah 6:3, Sanballat tries to stop Nehemiah from doing God's work. Nehemiah wisely replied, "I am doing a great work, and I cannot come down. Why should the work stop while I leave it and come down to you?"

If the critics have distracted you from doing God's work, here is a word to the wise.

Responding to your critics wastes time and energy. Focus on getting God's work done, and let the results silence the critics — instead of your work!

Today I will apply this wisdom in my life in the following ways:

_____

_____

To listen to this *Word to the Wise,* use your smart device to scan the QR code!

August 9

Love Can't Keep a Secret

John 14:23

It's been said, "If we love Christ, our devotion will not be made a secret." But just how will our love for Christ be revealed?

Jesus said in John 14:23, "If anyone loves Me, he will keep My Word, and My Father will love him, and We will come to him, and We will dwell with him."

If your love for Christ is still a secret, here is a word to the wise.

Our personal relationship with Christ is no private affair. If you love Christ, *show it* by learning and obeying His Word, because love can't keep a secret.

Today I will apply this wisdom in my life in the following ways:

_____

_____

To listen to this
Word to the Wise,
use your smart device
to scan the QR code!

August 10

Lover of Truth

Do you demand truth from others?

Are you dominated by truth? Conditions of the heart can be so filled with prejudice and bias that we are unwilling to listen to truth.

The Pharisees and the scribes were willing to receive teachings from their own people, but their hearts were not willing to receive Christ's instructions.

Are we like the Pharisees? And how are we any different? Here is a word to the wise.

As you conform yourself to the truth in the way you live, you'll go beyond what you ever thought was possible. Why? People are longing for truth, for something to believe in that's true and trustworthy. Therefore, trust in God's Word and be a lover of truth!

Today I will apply this wisdom in my life in the following ways:

_____

_____

To listen to this *Word to the Wise,* use your smart device to scan the QR code!

August 11

Education That Results in Devotion

I Timothy 1:5

Engraved on a small monument here at the College of Biblical Studies are Paul's words from I Timothy 1:5. It says, "The goal of our instruction is love."

Whenever the Bible is taught, believers should have one supreme goal – love.

If you feel like you need an added dose of love in your life, here is a word to the wise.

Listening to God's Word and studying God's Word, if done prayerfully in faith, will result in a greater appreciation of God's love and foster a greater love for Him in your heart. This will ensure an increased love for others. Don't merely look for an education – prayerfully seek an <u>ongoing</u> devotion.

Today I will apply this wisdom in my life in the following ways:

_____

_____

To listen to this
Word to the Wise,
use your smart device
to scan the QR code!

August 12

Recognize, Resist, and Remember

I Peter 5:8

In your Christian walk, have you ever noticed that the more serious you become in your commitment to Christ, the more your life gets interrupted by unsolicited problems, or so it seems?

For instance, a disturbing phone call at 2 a.m. or someone vandalizes your home while you're on vacation.

A.W. Tozer once said, "A Spirit-filled church will invite the anger of the enemy." This is probably why Peter in I Peter 5:8 says, "Be sober, be watchful, because your adversary, the devil, walks about like a roaring lion seeking whom he may devour."

Here is a word to the wise.

Ask God to help you recognize, resist, and then remember. *Recognize* the many signs of the adversary. *Resist* so you don't succumb to his attacks. And *remember*, when you get the victory, **God** gets the glory.

Today I will apply this wisdom in my life in the following ways:

To listen to this
Word to the Wise,
use your smart device
to scan the QR code!

The Devil Made Me Do It?

James 1:12-17

Most of us have heard the old excuse, "The devil made me do it." But have you ever said, "God made me this way?"

James 1:13-14 says, God does not tempt anyone, "but each one is tempted when he is carried away and enticed by his own desires."

If you wrestle with temptation, here is a word to the wise.

Don't blame God or the devil for your sin. Look to God for grace to overcome that temptation. James goes on to say that every good and perfect gift is from above, coming down from the Father. So, keep looking up! God is good **all** the time.

Today I will apply this wisdom in my life in the following ways:

_____

_____

To listen to this
Word to the Wise,
use your smart device
to scan the QR code!

August 14

A Wasted Life

Psalm 32:3

Eric Hoffer wrote, "We are warned not to waste time, but we are brought up to waste our lives."

A life of sin apart from Jesus Christ is the ultimate wasted life. Society portrays this as a good life, but ultimately, David portrays this as a groaning life. In Psalm 32:3, he says, "When I kept silent about my sin, my body wasted away through my groaning all day long."

If you are tired of wasting your life, here is a word to the wise.

Don't let sin squander away your life. Confess your sin today and make your life count.

Today I will apply this wisdom in my life in the following ways:

_____

_____

To listen to this
Word to the Wise,
use your smart device
to scan the QR code!

August 15

Behold, I Am with You

Genesis 28:15

Elizabeth Elliot said, "God has never promised to solve our problems. He has promised to go with us."

In Genesis 28, Jacob was running for his life because of his sin. God revealed Himself and made this promise: "Behold, I am with you and I will keep you wherever you go."

If problems in life have you on the run, here is a word to the wise.

Experiencing difficulties doesn't mean that God has forsaken you. Though Jacob's life had its share of pain, God blessed him through it all. Don't be so preoccupied with your temporal problems that you miss the privilege of enjoying ***His eternal presence***.

Today I will apply this wisdom in my life in the following ways:

_____

_____

To listen to this
Word to the Wise,
use your smart device
to scan the QR code!

August 16

Prayer Dead Zone

Matthew 6:15

Have you ever heard of the term "cellular dead zone"?

The term is often used when there is no communication signal between the service providers and your specific location. While you technically have coverage, there is something obstructing the signal.

Did you know that sometimes we can experience dead zones in our prayer life? Having an unforgiving spirit can obstruct the prayer connection between you and God. In Matthew 6:15, it says that if you refuse to forgive others, your Father will not forgive your sins.

Do you have a weak prayer signal? Here is a word to the wise.

Practice forgiveness daily. By forgiving those who have offended you, you will be removing your own dead zone.

Today I will apply this wisdom in my life in the following ways:

_____

_____

To listen to this
Word to the Wise,
use your smart device
to scan the QR code!

August 17

Be More Concerned About Your Faithfulness Than His

Psalm 34:4

When God gives us a goal, we think it is only natural for Him to help us succeed.

However, God often puts us in difficult and scary situations for us to experience His deliverance when we seek Him. Psalm 34:4 says, "I sought the Lord and He answered me and delivered me from all of my fears."

Do you think that God has left you alone on your journey? Here is a word to the wise.

Don't waste your spiritual or emotional energy worrying about the faithfulness of God. Rather, use this time by asking God to increase your own faithfulness to trust Him as He gives you the strength to finish the race.

Today I will apply this wisdom in my life in the following ways:

_____

_____

To listen to this
Word to the Wise,
use your smart device
to scan the QR code!

August 18

Secret to True Happiness

Proverbs 3:13

We're all familiar with the story of Solomon. God told him to ask for what he wanted.

Solomon asked for a discerning heart, and because of his faithfulness, we know him today as the wisest man that ever lived.

If you were given that same opportunity, what would you ask for? Matter of fact, what have you asked God for lately? Money? A new car? More stuff? Proverbs 3:13 says, "Happy is the man who finds wisdom and the man who gains understanding."

Here is a word to the wise.

The next time you talk to God, consider asking Him for wisdom and understanding, because true happiness can only be found in Christ.

Today I will apply this wisdom in my life in the following ways:

_____

_____

To listen to this
Word to the Wise,
use your smart device
to scan the QR code!

August 19

Smooth Talker

James 5:12

Once, a handshake was an adequate symbol of a man's integrity, but now, even legally binding contracts are regularly broken.

James 5:12 tells us, "Do not swear either by heaven or by earth or with any other oath, but let your yes be yes and your no be no so that you may not fall under judgment."

If you're not known for keeping your word, here is a word to the wise.

In the midst of life's trials, it is better to be a person of your word than a smooth talker. So, say what you mean and <u>mean what you say</u>.

Today I will apply this wisdom in my life in the following ways:

_____

_____

To listen to this
Word to the Wise,
use your smart device
to scan the QR code!

August 20

Who Cares?

Psalm 139:2

When we think about our relationship with God, sometimes our perception of Him is that He is far away in the clouds.

As Christians, at times we may question, "Does God love me or even care about what I do?" In Psalm 139:2, David says, "You know when I sit down and when I rise up." David is emphatically saying, "You know every move I make, and You are paying attention to my thoughts before I think them."

If you are doubtful about God's love towards you, here is a word to the wise.

God has not abandoned nor forsaken you. He loves you so much that He's not only watching over your every action, but He's also paying attention to your motivation. Now, that's a God who cares!

Today I will apply this wisdom in my life in the following ways:

_____

_____

To listen to this *Word to the Wise,* use your smart device to scan the QR code!

August 21

The Hope of Salvation

Ephesians 6:17

Did you know biblical hope is not merely wishful thinking, as we might say: "I hope I make it to work on time"? Biblical hope is confidence that what God has promised will come to pass.

In Ephesians 6:17, the apostle Paul calls believers to take the "helmet of salvation."

If you find yourself downcast in the spiritual battle, here is a word to the wise.

Remember the promise that God has given you through Christ Jesus, the gift of eternal salvation. So, the next time the enemy tries to rattle your thinking, don't make a wish. Hope in the reality of Jesus' return **for you** in glory.

Today I will apply this wisdom in my life in the following ways:

_____

_____

To listen to this
Word to the Wise,
use your smart device
to scan the QR code!

August 22

You Must Not Stay Silent

Proverbs 28:13

Have you ever wondered why most Christians don't confess their sins?

A first-century Roman politician, Seneca, provided a great answer when he said, "Because he is yet in them." Proverbs 28:13 says, "He who conceals his transgressions will not prosper, but he who confesses and forsakes them will find compassion."

Is the silence of your sin weighing you down? Here is a word to the wise.

Bring your sin out of darkness into the light by exposing it to God. After repenting, ask God to give you someone to hold you accountable. Make a commitment to righteous living, follow Jesus and walk in His marvelous light!

Today I will apply this wisdom in my life in the following ways:

_____

_____

To listen to this
Word to the Wise,
use your smart device
to scan the QR code!

August 23

Deck the Devil

James 4

A Chinese proverb says, "Quarreling is like cutting water with a sword." If quarreling doesn't accomplish anything except to make waves, why do we do it?

The book of James tells us that the root cause of our quarreling is personal desire. When we don't get what we want, we fight.

If you struggle with strife, here is a word to the wise.

James 4:7 says, "Resist the devil and he will flee from you. Humble yourselves in the presence of the Lord and He will exalt you." So submit your desires to God's will, and learn to pick the right fight. Don't deck the person! **Deck the devil** by drawing near to God in humble prayer.

Today I will apply this wisdom in my life in the following ways:

_____

_____

To listen to this
Word to the Wise,
use your smart device
to scan the QR code!

August 24

Help Me, God!

I Corinthians 13:7

Our popular wedding vows say, "For better or for worse, richer or poorer, in sickness and in health until death do us part, so help me God."

Unfortunately, for many, what they really mean is, "For better or *not so bad*, for richer or *a comfortable middle class, an occasional cold, or until I'm not happy*." First Corinthians 13:7 says that love "endures all things."

Are you struggling in your marriage? Here is a word to the wise.

Only God can sustain the love that endures all things. If you really want to improve your marriage, it's time for you to recognize that you can't do it under your own power – *so help me, God!*

Today I will apply this wisdom in my life in the following ways:

_____

_____

To listen to this
Word to the Wise,
use your smart device
to scan the QR code!

August 25

Sowing a Heap of Trouble

Galatians 6:7

If our actions are the seeds we plant, then our consequences are the crop we harvest.

There are earthly consequences and eternal consequences. You may feel like a certain behavior doesn't have immediate consequences, but sin always has consequences, and we will reap what we sow. It says in Galatians 6:7, "Do not be deceived. God is not mocked, for whatever a man sows, this he will also reap."

What are you sowing? Here is a word to the wise.

God allows us to make our own choices, but we must be prepared to deal with the consequences. Think before you act or you might be sowing a heap of trouble.

Today I will apply this wisdom in my life in the following ways:

_____

_____

To listen to this
Word to the Wise,
use your smart device
to scan the QR code!

August 26

Practice What You Preach

James 2:17

Have you ever heard the expression, "Put your money where your mouth is." You can talk a lot, but until you actually *do* it, it's just that — a bunch of talk.

James 2:17 says, "Even so, faith without works is dead."

If you're wondering how to best tell others about your faith, here is a word to the wise.

A person's claim of faith is eventually evidenced by what he does. Abraham trusted God so he offered up Isaac. Rahab believed in the true God so she protected His messengers. If you say you trust in Christ, show it by how you live your life.

Today I will apply this wisdom in my life in the following ways:

_____

_____

To listen to this
Word to the Wise,
use your smart device
to scan the QR code!

August 27

Where Are You, God?

Exodus 3:7

Do you know how much God loves you?

In times of suffering, we may think that God does not care. The Israelites probably thought this during their enslavement in Egypt. Contrary to their belief, God was making plans for their rescue. According to Exodus 3:7, the Lord said, "I have surely seen the affliction of My people who are in Egypt and have given heed to their cry because of their taskmasters, so I am aware of their suffering."

Have you ever said, "God, where are You?" in your time of trouble? Here is a word to the wise.

While you may think in your time of suffering that God does not care, be patient. He may be making preparation for _**your**_ deliverance!

Today I will apply this wisdom in my life in the following ways:

_____

_____

To listen to this
Word to the Wise,
use your smart device
to scan the QR code!

August 28

No Compromise – Even Under Fire

Daniel 3

In Daniel Chapter 3, Nebuchadnezzar said to Shadrach, Meshach, and Abednego, "If you don't worship my god, you'll be cast into a burning fiery furnace."

In the face of a fiery death, the three Hebrew boys responded by saying, "Our God whom we serve is able to deliver us. But even if He does not, be it known to you, O king, that we will not serve your god or worship the golden image that you have set up."

Are you living a life without compromise? Here is a word to the wise.

Ask God to give you the fortitude to say no to the pressures of this world and no to your own sinful desires. "No" means <u>no compromise</u> – even under fire!

Today I will apply this wisdom in my life in the following ways:

_____

_____

To listen to this
Word to the Wise,
use your smart device
to scan the QR code!

August 29

In His Hands

Genesis 19:15-16

It's been said, "Those who will not deliver themselves into the hands of God's mercy cannot be delivered out of the hands of His justice."

In Genesis 19, Lot hesitated to leave Sodom when the angels warned him of the coming judgment. Incredibly, the heavenly messengers led Lot and his family out of the city by the hand.

If you've ever hesitated in the face of incredible mercy, here is a word to the wise.

Love for the comforts of this world is both powerful and deluding, but if you are a believer, God's faithful love is greater still. We all know what happened to Lot's wife. Don't look back! Place yourself in the merciful hand of God.

Today I will apply this wisdom in my life in the following ways:

To listen to this
Word to the Wise,
use your smart device
to scan the QR code!

August 30

That Tiny Crack in the Windshield

James 5:20

Sin is like a crack in your windshield.

If you deal with it quickly, you can keep it from spreading, but if you don't fix it soon, it will spread to your entire windshield and will cost you more to repair it.

James 5:20 says, "He who turns a sinner from the error of his ways will save his soul from death and will cover a multitude of sins."

Do you know someone who is drowning in sin? Here is a word to the wise.

Getting someone to turn away and repent not only saves them from that particular sin, but also the possibility of other unconfessed sins from spreading.

Today I will apply this wisdom in my life in the following ways:

_____

_____

To listen to this
Word to the Wise,
use your smart device
to scan the QR code!

Answer Man

John 6:68

One theologian said, "Better a baffled faith than no faith at all."

In John 6, we read of a time when many of Jesus' would-be disciples withdrew and were not walking with Him anymore. Why? Because He didn't meet their expectations.

If you've ever felt confused, disappointed, and wanted to walk away from your commitment to Christ, here is a word to the wise.

Peter offers a sobering response when he says in John 6:68, "Lord, to whom shall we go? You have the words of eternal life." Keep the faith even when you don't understand. Jesus still has all the answers!

Today I will apply this wisdom in my life in the following ways:

_____

_____

To listen to this
Word to the Wise,
use your smart device
to scan the QR code!

September 1

Beauty in the Eye of the Beholder

Psalm 33:1

With all the emphasis today on external beauty, there has been a great increase in cosmetic surgery, fitness routines, and special diets.

Some of that may be fine, but the key to beauty is found in Psalm 33:1. It says, "Rejoice in the Lord, you righteous ones. Praise from the upright is beautiful."

If you are struggling to be more attractive, here is a word to the wise.

Praise to Christ for His righteousness and grace is **absolutely stunning** to God! Rejoice in Jesus and you will find that beauty is found in the eye of the One who beholds Himself in you.

Today I will apply this wisdom in my life in the following ways:

_____

_____

To listen to this
Word to the Wise,
use your smart device
to scan the QR code!

September 2

Harvesting the Fruit

Galatians 6:9

In the midst of our busy lives, it's easy to become tired of doing good.

As Christians, we get tired of serving at work, at church, and even at home. Sometimes we think, "Let someone else do good. I quit!" But in Galatians 6:9, it says, "Let us not lose heart in doing good for, in due time, we will reap if we do not grow weary."

Are you getting tired? Here is a word to the wise.

Even the best do-gooders get frustrated, but they never stop. Why? Because doing good soon produces its own **good fruit**!

Today I will apply this wisdom in my life in the following ways:

_____

_____

To listen to this
Word to the Wise,
use your smart device
to scan the QR code!

September 3

Never-Ending Vacation

Proverbs 14:13

Someone said, "Laughter is an instant vacation."

While laughter is a great gift from God, it never seems to permanently alter the difficult realities we face. Proverbs 14:13 says, "Laughter can conceal a heavy heart, but when the laughter ends, the grief remains."

If your vacation is quickly coming to an end, here is a word to the wise.

The Bible declares in God's presence there is fullness of joy. Stop settling for temporary vacations. Keep your focus on your relationship with Christ and the glorious joy that never ends.

Today I will apply this wisdom in my life in the following ways:

_____

_____

To listen to this
Word to the Wise,
use your smart device
to scan the QR code!

September 4

Where Is Your Hope?

Psalm 42:5

Sometimes we are too prone to *listen* to ourselves when we should be *talking* to ourselves.

In Psalm 42, David began talking to himself in order to combat what he was hearing from his heart. Twice he said, "Why are you so in despair, oh my soul, and why have you become disturbed within me? Hope in God."

If you've ever heard the voice of hopelessness whispering in your heart, here is a word to the wise.

Don't linger over feelings of despair. Counsel yourself in the Word of God. Your hope is neither in your feelings nor in your circumstances. **Your hope is in the Living God who is your life**.

Today I will apply this wisdom in my life in the following ways:

_____

_____

To listen to this
Word to the Wise,
use your smart device
to scan the QR code!

September 5

Are You Looking for Trouble?

Proverbs 15:6

We've all heard the old saying, "Money can't buy happiness."

Is that even in the Bible? Well, not in those exact words, but Proverbs 15:6 says, "Great wealth is in the house of the righteous, but trouble is in the income of the wicked."

So what does that mean? Great wealth is in the house of the righteous? Let's face it. Not every righteous person has money. The context here indicates that the opposite of wealth is trouble, thus wealth refers to peace or happiness.

Here is a word to the wise.

If you think money is the key to happiness, you're looking for trouble. Walk with God. He alone is the source of true happiness.

Today I will apply this wisdom in my life in the following ways:

_____

_____

To listen to this *Word to the Wise*, use your smart device to scan the QR code!

September 6

Free Indeed
John 8:31

One writer has said, "The only freedom that man ever has is when he becomes a slave to Jesus Christ." Is that really true?

Jesus said in John 8, "Everyone who practices sin is a slave to sin," but He promised, "If you continue in My Word, you are truly My disciples and you will know the truth and the truth will make you free."

If you want to be free from sin's bondage, here is a word to the wise.

Trust Christ and continue in His teachings. He frees the believer from the punishment of sin, the power of sin, and one day, even the very presence of sin.

Today I will apply this wisdom in my life in the following ways:

_____

_____

To listen to this
Word to the Wise,
use your smart device
to scan the QR code!

Where Is God?

I Kings 19:11-13

Do you ever find yourself asking, "God, where are You?" because you can't feel God?

Are you spiraling into depression, perhaps even struggling with atheism?

So many of us are looking for assurance in the dramatic. Even Elijah looked for assurance in the dramatic after he left Mount Carmel, but God did not speak in that manner. Instead, God responded in a still, small voice.

Here is a word to the wise.

Don't look for the assurance in the dramatic. Instead, get out of the rat race, find a quiet place to pray, **and that's where you'll find God**!

Today I will apply this wisdom in my life in the following ways:

_____

_____

To listen to this
Word to the Wise,
use your smart device
to scan the QR code!

Follow the Instructions

Psalm 111:10

Sometimes in life I struggle with following instructions or directions.

I just cannot surrender to the manufacturer's way of putting a product together.

Did you know that following God's instructions is the beginning of wisdom? Psalms 111:10 says, "The fear of the Lord is the beginning of wisdom." If we desire to grow in wisdom, we must also surrender our will completely to the authority of God.

Here is a word to the wise.

Ask God to show you the areas in your life where you're not willing to follow His instructions. Confess it, surrender it, and live it.

Today I will apply this wisdom in my life in the following ways:

_____

_____

To listen to this
Word to the Wise,
use your smart device
to scan the QR code!

252

September 9

Wisdom of a Humble Response

Ecclesiastes 10:4

Have you ever done or said something rash at work only to regret it later, perhaps even jeopardizing your employment status?

Ecclesiastes 10:4 warns us, "If your boss is angry at you, don't quit. A quiet spirit can overcome even great mistakes."

If you have ever been tempted to lose your head, here is a word to the wise.

Whether you are at fault or your boss is at fault, don't impulsively throw away the relationship or the job for a momentary feeling. A humble response can overcome a heated exchange. Keep your head and employ a quiet spirit, or you may be headed to the unemployment line.

Today I will apply this wisdom in my life in the following ways:

_____

_____

To listen to this
Word to the Wise,
use your smart device
to scan the QR code!

September 10

Christ Alone

Genesis 9:21

Did you know that even righteous Noah was a sinner? Genesis 9:20-21 reveals that after the flood he planted a vineyard and became drunk with the wine he produced. If Noah was susceptible to sin, is there any hope for us?

Here is a word to the wise.

There's only one man who never sinned and always did what was right – Jesus Christ, God in human flesh. God has promised to forgive and justify all those who trust in Christ's righteousness and not their own.

It's okay to respect godly people, but don't be surprised by the sin of others. Keep looking to Christ. He alone is righteous. He alone will save!

Today I will apply this wisdom in my life in the following ways:

_____

_____

To listen to this *Word to the Wise,* use your smart device to scan the QR code!

Weariness Will Give Way to Worship

Hebrews 10:36

Sometimes the promises of Scripture seem so distant.

We have all felt that feeling of spiritual tiredness when everything we see and experience in this world seems to cast a shadow on the faith realities we believe.

Hebrews 10:36 says, "… you need to persevere so that, when you have done the will of God, you will receive what He has promised."

If you are sensing weariness in your faith, here is a word to the wise.

Look to Jesus who, for the joy set before Him, endured the cross and now sits at the right hand of the Father. There is coming a day when your weariness really will give way to worship!

Today I will apply this wisdom in my life in the following ways:

_____

_____

To listen to this
Word to the Wise,
use your smart device
to scan the QR code!

September 12

Don't Worry, Be Happy!

Psalm 1:1-2

If someone asks you what the path to true happiness is, what would you tell them?

Some believe the pathway to happiness is found in education or wealth. Others believe it to be in marriage or family. So, what is the path to true happiness?

Here is a word to the wise.

Psalm 1:1 indicates that, "Happy is the man that does not walk with the wicked nor stand with the sinner or sit in the seat of the scoffers, but his delight is in the law of the Lord." To find lasting happiness, you must learn to delight in God's Word. So stop worrying, open God's Word, and be happy!

Today I will apply this wisdom in my life in the following ways:

_____

_____

To listen to this
Word to the Wise,
use your smart device
to scan the QR code!

Never Be Ashamed to Serve

II Timothy 1:16-18

Have you ever been hesitant to minister to someone enduring shameful circumstances?

Some believers in Paul's day were embarrassed to associate with him because he was too outspoken and in prison for it. However, there were a faithful few who sought him out and ministered to him.

If someone's embarrassing circumstances are making you hesitant to reach out to them, here is a word to the wise.

In II Timothy 1, Paul prayed for God's blessings on Onesiphorus because he cared for Paul in his time of need. Be discerning, but never let this be a cover for your own hesitation. Never be ashamed to help a brother in need.

Today I will apply this wisdom in my life in the following ways:

_____

_____

To listen to this
Word to the Wise,
use your smart device
to scan the QR code!

 *Word* to the **Wise**

September 14

Gangsters, Goody-Two-Shoes, and Grace

Titus 3:5

As the President of the College of Biblical Studies, I am constantly amazed by the testimony of our students to the grace of God.

We have a diverse student body, students who come from all walks of life. Some came to know the Lord as children; others, in prison.

If the grace of God has become more of a theological concept to you than truly amazing, here is a word to the wise.

Titus 3 reminds us He saved us not on the basis of deeds which we have done in righteousness, but according to His mercy and grace. So, whether you're a gangster or a goody-two-shoes, salvation is all about *grace*.

Today I will apply this wisdom in my life in the following ways:

_____

_____

To listen to this
Word to the Wise,
use your smart device
to scan the QR code!

September 15

Prescription for Prayer

James 5:13

A group of physicians decided to conduct a blind study to determine the efficacy of Christian prayer on healing. The results demonstrated that patients who were prayed for suffered less congestive heart failure, had fewer episodes of pneumonia, and had fewer cardiac arrests.

Therefore, it is no surprise that the Bible instructs us in James to pray when we are suffering, and when we are too weak, to ask others to pray on our behalf.

If you need to experience peace in your troubling situation, here is a word to the wise.

God's wisdom compels us to call on Him. No matter your circumstances, prayer is the pathway to peace in Jesus!

Today I will apply this wisdom in my life in the following ways:

_____

_____

To listen to this
Word to the Wise,
use your smart device
to scan the QR code!

Sin's Boomerang

Genesis 29:25-28

We've all heard the expression, "What goes around comes around."

Though the Bible reveals that sometimes this is not the case, in Genesis 29, Jacob, the deceiver, was blindsided by deception. He was tricked into marrying two sisters and becoming an indentured servant for fourteen years.

If you're suffering from the boomerang effects of sin, here is a word to the wise.

God's presence and protection does not mean that you will never feel the sting of sin, but He will accompany you through everything that you go through. Praise God, what goes around does not *always* come around, but when it does, He is with you and perfecting you through it all!

Today I will apply this wisdom in my life in the following ways:

_____

_____

To listen to this
Word to the Wise,
use your smart device
to scan the QR code!

September 17

Shine On!

John 12:27

Have you ever noticed that trouble has no problem finding us?

It seems like it comes out of thin air. Unfortunately, there's not a living soul that is exempt from trouble. Even Jesus experienced trouble. But look at His perspective in John 12:27. He said, "Now My soul is troubled, but what shall I say? Father, save Me from this hour? No, on the contrary. For this purpose I have come to this hour."

Are you currently in a whirlwind? Is your life spiraling out of control? Here is a word to the wise.

It may not be God's will to take you out of your troubling situation, but to have you shine all the way through it!

Today I will apply this wisdom in my life in the following ways:

_____

_____

To listen to this
Word to the Wise,
use your smart device
to scan the QR code!

September 18

Finding Satisfaction

Proverbs 25:16

Have you ever heard the expression, "You can have too much of a good thing"?

Proverbs 25:16 says, "If you find honey, eat just enough. Too much of it and you will vomit."

If you've ever felt that sick feeling after indulging a bit too much, here is a word to the wise.

Ever since the fall, man has sought to find satisfaction in God's gifts rather than in God Himself. Pursue Christ. The more you do, the more you'll be satisfied. You can never get too much of God. Why? Because He is infinitely and eternally good.

Today I will apply this wisdom in my life in the following ways:

_____

_____

To listen to this
Word to the Wise,
use your smart device
to scan the QR code!

Practice Before You Preach

Luke 6:39

We have often heard the statement, "Practice what you preach."

Oftentimes, this is used of a hypocrite who says one thing, but does another. In order to guide others into truth, we must first be able to proclaim a truth that we have actually experienced so we can model it to others.

If you are guilty of pointing out a truth to others and not following it yourself, here is a word to the wise.

Jesus said in Luke 6:39, "A blind man cannot lead another blind man without both falling into the pit." Ask God today to help you start practicing **before** you preach.

Today I will apply this wisdom in my life in the following ways:

_____

_____

To listen to this
Word to the Wise,
use your smart device
to scan the QR code!

September 20

Flood Insurance

Proverbs 17:14

If we are created to be relational beings, why is it so painful for us to be in relationships?

One word – conflict.

Conflicts are like credit card debt. It's easy to get in, but hard to get out. Are your relationships flooded by conflicts? Proverbs 17:14 says, "To start a conflict is to release a flood. Stop the dispute before it breaks out."

Here is a word to the wise.

The best way to stop a flood is to make sure your levies are secure. Ask God to calm your heart and hold your tongue or you may find yourself drowning in a long, painful relationship.

Today I will apply this wisdom in my life in the following ways:

_____

_____

To listen to this
Word to the Wise,
use your smart device
to scan the QR code!

September 21

When All Hope Is Lost

Lamentations 3:18-23

Have you ever suffered because of someone else's sin?

The prophet Jeremiah had to live through unspeakable horrors because of the sins of others. How did he handle such suffering? In Lamentations 3, the prophet prayed, "Remember my affliction. The Lord's lovingkindness never ceases for His compassions never fail. They are new every morning."

If you are suffering because of someone else, here is a word to the wise.

Don't hopelessly dwell on *their* folly. Ask the Lord to remember your affliction and cry out to Him, "Great is thy faithfulness!"

Today I will apply this wisdom in my life in the following ways:

_____

_____

To listen to this *Word to the Wise,* use your smart device to scan the QR code!

You're Still in the Game

Acts 23-28

Do you ever feel like God has you on the sidelines and you can't figure out why you are not in the game?

According to the book of Acts, the apostle Paul, the greatest missionary in history, was imprisoned for two years in Caesarea and another two years in Rome.

If you are wondering why you are not being allowed the opportunity to fully use your giftedness, here is a word to the wise.

During those years in prison, Paul actually wrote many of his New Testament letters that have blessed billions of people throughout history. So stop worrying about what you can't do right now, and do what you can do. As long as you are breathing, you are still in the game.

Today I will apply this wisdom in my life in the following ways:

_____

_____

To listen to this
Word to the Wise,
use your smart device
to scan the QR code!

Do I Have to Forgive?

Matthew 6:15

Did you know that people who have difficulty forgiving are more prone to physical illnesses?

This may be related to what Jesus said in Matthew 6:15: "But if you do not forgive others their trespasses, neither will your Father forgive *your* trespasses."

Do you have a forgiveness condition? Here is help. Write down the names of those people who make it almost impossible for you to forgive. Pray and ask God to help you remember the Matthew 6:15 principle: "I must forgive if I want to be forgiven."

Here is a word to the wise.

Be obedient to God's Word. Start forgiving and start living.

Today I will apply this wisdom in my life in the following ways:

_____

_____

To listen to this
Word to the Wise,
use your smart device
to scan the QR code!

September 24

What Fills Your Heart?

Proverbs 12:20

One writer has said, "The plans you shape, shape you."

What we think about ultimately shapes who we are.

Proverbs 12:20 says, "Deceit fills hearts that are plotting evil; joy fills hearts that are planning peace."

Here is a question for you. What fills your heart? Here is a word to the wise.

Make plans to exalt Christ and promote His peace through the gospel. The more the Scriptures shape your thinking, the more like Christ you will become. The more you become like Christ, the more joy you'll have. Let go of your deception and find your satisfaction in Christ.

Today I will apply this wisdom in my life in the following ways:

_____

_____

To listen to this
Word to the Wise,
use your smart device
to scan the QR code!

Winds of Change

John 3:1-21

Have you ever seen the wind?

Jesus said in John 3:8, "The wind blows where it wishes, and you hear the sound of it but do not know where it comes from and where it is going; so is everyone who is born of the Spirit."

If you are seeing no sign of a spiritual breeze in your life, here is a word to the wise.

Just as the wind is under God's sovereign control and cannot be seen except for its effects, so is the new birth. God sovereignly regenerates those who trust in His Son, and then His Spirit is forever influencing them. If you desire a new birth, ask God for the winds of change in Christ!

Today I will apply this wisdom in my life in the following ways:

_____

_____

To listen to this
Word to the Wise,
use your smart device
to scan the QR code!

No Regrets

Proverbs 5

What governs your actual decision-making?

Is it a feeling of happiness or satisfaction, gratification of the senses, recreation, or amusement?

Solomon explains in Proverbs 5 that there are two types of pleasures, namely, false pleasures and true pleasures. False pleasures are illegitimate gratification that will extract the best parts of your soul, whereas true pleasures can mightily enrich your life.

Are you engaged in pleasures that zap your life? Here is a word to the wise.

By knowing and living out God's Word, you will be free from the perils of false pleasures. Study God's Word to live a life **with no regret**!

Today I will apply this wisdom in my life in the following ways:

_____

_____

To listen to this
Word to the Wise,
use your smart device
to scan the QR code!

Peace Be with You

Mark 14:50; John 20:19

On the night of Jesus' betrayal, all of His disciples pledged their willingness to die with Him. But when He was arrested, and they saw Jesus' refusal to resist, Mark 14:50 says, "They all left Him and fled."

If you've ever felt the shame of failing to stand up for Jesus, here is a word to the wise.

The failed disciples did not permanently abandon Christ *because Christ had not abandoned them.* Rather, His response after the resurrection was, "Peace be with you."

Confess your fear and shame to Him and His peace will be with you, too. He never abandons His own.

Today I will apply this wisdom in my life in the following ways:

_____

_____

To listen to this *Word to the Wise,* use your smart device to scan the QR code!

September 28

Keep On, Keepin' On

Exodus 5

Do you ever think you are doing what God has called you to do only to see your circumstances get worse?

In Exodus 5, Moses was clearly obeying God's will in calling Pharaoh to let Israel go. Yet, Pharaoh only made Israel's labor more grievous. As you would expect, both Israel and Moses were upset that things were now more difficult.

Are you tempted to bail out on obedience because it seems to be making things worse? Here is a word to the wise.

If you're clearly obeying God's Word, you're not making things worse. No matter how it seems, keep on doing what God commands, and like Israel, you will one day see the deliverance of the Lord.

Today I will apply this wisdom in my life in the following ways:

_____

_____

To listen to this
Word to the Wise,
use your smart device
to scan the QR code!

September 29

God's Five-Star Rating

Galatians 1:10

In today's world, approval ratings are everything, so they say.

Did you know that seeking approval of men can be dangerous to your spiritual growth? Paul said in Galatians 1:10, "For am I seeking favor of men or of God, or am I striving to please men? If I were still trying to please men, I would not be found a bond-servant of Christ."

Who is your source of approval in life? God? Or people? Here is a word to the wise.

Paul says you cannot effectively serve God while trying to get approval of men. Ask God to help you seek His approval in all that you do. Truly, He is the only one that can keep you and your approval rating from falling.

Today I will apply this wisdom in my life in the following ways:

_____

_____

To listen to this *Word to the Wise*, use your smart device to scan the QR code!

September 30

I Hear the Train Coming

Proverbs 3:5

When speaking about persevering in faith in spite of the extreme trials she faced, Corrie Ten Boom said, "When a train goes through a tunnel and it gets dark, you don't throw away your ticket and jump off. You sit still and trust the engineer."

If you sometimes feel like jumping off the train in the midst of your trials, here is a word to the wise.

Proverbs 3:5 issues the command to God's people, "Trust in the Lord with all your heart and don't lean on your own understanding." Never let your feelings control your fidelity to God's Word. Keep walking in obedience, waiting for His deliverance. The train will eventually arrive at its glorious destination.

Today I will apply this wisdom in my life in the following ways:

_____

_____

To listen to this
Word to the Wise,
use your smart device
to scan the QR code!

October 1

It's All About Grace

Genesis 1:1; Revelation 22:21

Most of us have heard something about and used the word "grace," but what is grace?

Perhaps a good illustration of grace is that of an infant who is completely dependent upon his parents' goodwill to live. Grace is the loving care of an infinitely good and kind God toward those who are utterly helpless.

If you have never thought of grace quite like that, here is a word to the wise.

Genesis starts with "In the beginning God created," and Revelation ends with "May the grace of the Lord Jesus be with you all." From the beginning to the end, life is all about grace. **Praise God for His grace in Jesus!**

Today I will apply this wisdom in my life in the following ways:

_____

_____

To listen to this
Word to the Wise,
use your smart device
to scan the QR code!

275

October 2

Lies for Sale!

Proverbs 23:23

Winston Churchill said, "A lie gets halfway around the world before the truth has a chance to get its pants on."

Most of the time, we don't regard deception or small lies for what they really are – lies. "I'm ten minutes away"; "I'm not in that much pain"; or, here's my favorite, "Everything's okay. I'm really doing fine." God wants us to keep truth at the forefront of our mouths.

According to Proverbs 23:23, the Bible says, "Buy truth and don't sell it. Get wisdom and instruction and understanding."

Here is a word to the wise.

Stock up on the truth of God's Word and stop selling lies.

Today I will apply this wisdom in my life in the following ways:

_____

_____

To listen to this
Word to the Wise,
use your smart device
to scan the QR code!

October 3

Superficial Seeker or Sinner Saved by Grace?

Luke 18-19

Have you ever noticed the intriguing flow of thought in the Gospel narratives?

One example is found in Luke Chapters 18 and 19. In Chapter 18, we read about the rich young ruler and his decision not to follow Jesus. In Chapter 19, Jesus heals a blind beggar who follows Him; then, our Lord saves a wealthy Zacchaeus.

What is the difference between these men? Here is a word to the wise.

Two of them saw the value of knowing and following Christ as more important than anything else. The other did not. However, this is more than a literary lesson. Superficial seeker or sinner who wants to follow Jesus — which one are you?

Today I will apply this wisdom in my life in the following ways:

_____

_____

To listen to this
Word to the Wise,
use your smart device
to scan the QR code!

October 4

Brrr!

Proverbs 12:18

It's been said that the warmth of the sun will compel a man to take off his coat, whereas the cold winds make him wrap it around him more tightly. Are your words a blustery wind or a burst of sunshine?

Proverbs 12:18 says, "There is one who speaks rashly like the thrusts of a sword, But the tongue of the wise brings healing."

If your tongue is causing your relationships trouble, here is a word to the wise.

The next time you feel tempted to speak coldly or to cut someone to the quick, make sure your tongue is neither a blustery wind nor a slashing sword. Speak the words that reflect the S-O-N who brings healing in His wings!

Today I will apply this wisdom in my life in the following ways:

_____

_____

To listen to this
Word to the Wise,
use your smart device
to scan the QR code!

The Only Cure for Our Corruption

Genesis 3

Someone has said, "The history of man is his attempt to escape his own corruption."

Adam and Eve hid from God in an attempt to somehow avoid the consequences of sin. If we're honest with ourselves in our own lives, we have been marked by the desire to avoid the consequences of our sin without facing up to our own inner corruption.

So, what's the answer? Here is a word to the wise.

Jesus Christ vicariously took on our corruption so that we could escape its eternal consequences. Recognize your sin and embrace the only Savior of corrupt sinners – **Jesus**.

Today I will apply this wisdom in my life in the following ways:

_____

_____

To listen to this
Word to the Wise,
use your smart device
to scan the QR code!

October 6

Key to a Relationship That Will Never End

John 1:1; Romans 5:8

What is the first thing that must happen in any relationship? Communication. Did you know that God has spoken to us?

In John Chapter 1, it says, "In the beginning was the Word and the Word was with God and the Word was God. And the Word became flesh and dwelt among us." Romans 5:8 says, "God demonstrated His own love toward us in that while we were yet sinners Christ died for us."

If you have not responded to God's communication and perfect love, here is a word to the wise.

Open your heart to receive what God is saying to you through His Word. Why? Because He's looking for a relationship that will never end.

Today I will apply this wisdom in my life in the following ways:

_____

_____

To listen to this
Word to the Wise,
use your smart device
to scan the QR code!

October 7

Did You Put God on Hold?

Psalm 66:18

Do you ever feel at times that your prayers are not being answered?

Believe it or not, there are some obstacles that can hinder our prayer process. Sin that is not confessed will short-circuit your prayer life. In Psalm 66:18, it says, "If I regard wickedness in my heart, the Lord will not hear."

Do you have any unconfessed sin? Here is a word to the wise.

Genuine confession is not only good for the soul, but also, it's good for getting God's attention. So, if you haven't heard from God in a while, He might be waiting to hear a good word from you!

Today I will apply this wisdom in my life in the following ways:

_____

_____

To listen to this
Word to the Wise,
use your smart device
to scan the QR code!

October 8

"Check Engine" Light

Genesis 14:12

Have you ever chosen to ignore the *"Check Engine"* light on your car's dashboard?

In Genesis 14, three foreign armies captured all the people and property of Sodom, including Lot, his family, and all that they owned. In grace, God enabled Abraham to defeat the invaders and rescue Lot, saving his property and wealth. Instead of heeding the warning, Lot resumed his life in Sodom.

If you've been ignoring your *"Check Life"* light, here is a word to the wise.

When faced with the need to change, don't shrug it off. Turn to the Word of God and the promises of prayer. Get out that owner's manual and call God for help!

Today I will apply this wisdom in my life in the following ways:

_____

_____

To listen to this
Word to the Wise,
use your smart device
to scan the QR code!

How Does God See Your Sin?

Romans 7:19

William Shakespeare said, "Few love to hear the sins they love to act."

Sometimes the sin we detest most in others is the very sin we regularly commit.

In Romans 7:19, Paul says, "For the good that I want, I do not do, but I practice the very evil that I do not want."

If you're guilty of criticizing others for the same sin you commit yourself, here is a word to the wise.

Ask God to show you your sin as He sees it. This humbling process creates a hatred for our own sin while showing compassion toward others who share in the same struggle.

Today I will apply this wisdom in my life in the following ways:

_____

_____

To listen to this
Word to the Wise,
use your smart device
to scan the QR code!

October 10

Heaping Helping of Love

Proverbs 15:17

Assuming you're not a vegan, would you rather have a serving of broccoli, spinach, and radishes or a T-bone steak with all the fixings?

Before you answer, consider Proverbs 15:17. "Better is a dish of vegetables where love is than a fatted oxen served with hatred."

Have you ever felt unloved in the midst of creature comforts? Here is a word to the wise.

Learn to cultivate biblical relationships with others rather than chasing after creature comforts. Serve and care for your friends as you walk with Christ and you will find lasting comfort. Even if you're a vegan, a berry and spinach smoothie is sweeter with a whole lot of loving.

Today I will apply this wisdom in my life in the following ways:

_____

_____

To listen to this
Word to the Wise,
use your smart device
to scan the QR code!

October 11

Suffering Has a Purpose

Romans 5:3-4

Have you ever experienced a difficult time in your life when you felt hopeless and helpless?

Are you in a crisis currently and you feel like giving up? Maybe because of the loss of a loved one, a rebellious child, or a devastating divorce. Is there hope?

Yes. Suffering has a purpose. Paul writes in Romans 5:3-4, "And we know that suffering produces perseverance, perseverance character, and character hope."

Here is a word to the wise.

Ask God to show you what He desires to develop in you through this crisis. Then, ask for patience while the Master goes to work.

Today I will apply this wisdom in my life in the following ways:

_____

_____

To listen to this
Word to the Wise,
use your smart device
to scan the QR code!

October 12

Trouble-Free Future Ahead

Proverbs 12:21

Proverbs 12:21 says, "No harm befalls the righteous, but the wicked are filled with trouble."

How can you reconcile this with the lives of Job, Paul, or Jesus? They were right with God, yet they experienced great trouble in this life.

Here is a word to the wise.

These are exceptions to the proverbial wisdom in this fallen world. Though we can at times suffer trouble because of our sin, we may also face trouble even when we haven't sinned. Because God causes all things to work together for the good of those who love Him, keep trusting God's promises. There is a trouble-free future ahead.

Today I will apply this wisdom in my life in the following ways:

_____

_____

To listen to this
Word to the Wise,
use your smart device
to scan the QR code!

Learn His Voice

John 10:27

On one family retreat, we played a game, "Follow the Voice to the Treasure."

One person was a good voice; the other, the evil; and the last was the follower. The good voice will lead them to the treasure, but the evil voice will lead them astray. The follower has to decide whose voice he will follow. Their choice will ultimately determine if they find the treasure.

Whose voice do you follow? Jesus says in John 10:27, "My sheep hear My voice and I know them and they follow Me."

Here is a word to the wise.

God speaks through His Word, so read it and learn His voice.

Today I will apply this wisdom in my life in the following ways:

_____

_____

To listen to this
Word to the Wise,
use your smart device
to scan the QR code!

October 14

Your Opinion Matters

Mark 6

Horatius Bonar said, "In all unbelief there are two things – a good opinion of oneself and a bad opinion of God."

In Mark 6, the people in Jesus' hometown heard His teachings and of His power, but they were skeptical that He was really more than just the local carpenter whose family they knew. Jesus marveled at their unbelief.

If you've ever questioned Jesus' power to work in your life, here is a word to the wise.

Trust Jesus to give you whatever is best, whether miraculous healing or difficult but faithful endurance. Be wary of your own opinion of yourself and your situation, and believe God for His perfect provision.

Today I will apply this wisdom in my life in the following ways:

_____

_____

To listen to this
Word to the Wise,
use your smart device
to scan the QR code!

288

October 15

Devastation and Divine Revelation

Daniel 10:16-18

Have you ever felt God's peace and refreshment after a quiet time in the Scriptures?

We're not always aware, however, of the toll it took on those who recorded what God had revealed.

In Chapter 10 of Daniel, he wrote, "As a result of the vision, anguish has come upon me and I have retained no strength, nor has any breath been left in me." Much of the chapter speaks of the devastating effects of divine revelation.

Here is a word to the wise.

The Bible is not just a feel-good devotional. Yes, it can and should bring peace, refreshment, and freedom. But never forget the sobering reality — it is the very Word of God.

Today I will apply this wisdom in my life in the following ways:

_____

_____

To listen to this
Word to the Wise,
use your smart device
to scan the QR code!

October 16

Susanna, *Who?*

Luke 8:3

Do you remember Susanna in the Bible?

In Luke 8:3, Susanna is mentioned by name as one of those who helped finance the ministry of Jesus and His disciples.

It also says that there were "many others who were contributing to their support out of their private means."

Here is a word to the wise.

Even today there are ministries that are faithfully carrying out the ministry of Jesus. As president of the College of Biblical Studies, everyday I see how such financial support is vital to the gospel ministry. Prayerfully and joyfully, remember to support the ministry of God's Word. God remembers those who do.

Today I will apply this wisdom in my life in the following ways:

_____

_____

To listen to this
Word to the Wise,
use your smart device
to scan the QR code!

October 17

What's Mastering You?

Numbers 20:10

Have you ever heard the saying, "It's like herding cats"?

People who don't master their emotions have a difficult time holding their peace.

Moses in Numbers 20:10 had a problem mastering his emotions. Matter of fact, he said to the people, "Listen now, you rebels, shall we bring forth water out of this rock?" And he hit the rock, which God did not command him to do.

Do you have a problem mastering your emotions? Here is a word to the wise.

Ask God to master your emotions, or your emotions will certainly master you!

Today I will apply this wisdom in my life in the following ways:

_____

_____

To listen to this
Word to the Wise,
use your smart device
to scan the QR code!

October 18

Peace, Justice, and Prosperity

Micah 4:1-5

What are some universal desires of mankind? Peace? Justice? Prosperity?

Micah 4 tells us that in the last days peace, justice, and prosperity will indeed be realized when God Himself comes to rule the world.

If you're longing for these, here is a word to the wise.

Micah 4:5 says, "Though the nations around us follow their idols, we will follow the Lord our God forever and ever." If you really believe in God's promises for the future, live for Christ now and enjoy real peace, justice, and prosperity forever.

Today I will apply this wisdom in my life in the following ways:

_____

_____

To listen to this
Word to the Wise,
use your smart device
to scan the QR code!

Chains of Love

John 18:6-12

Have you ever thought about the cords that bound Jesus as He was arrested the night before His crucifixion?

In John 18:12, it says, "The Roman cohort and the commander and the officers of the Jews arrested Jesus *and bound Him.*" Just moments before the arrest, Jesus had announced that He is the I AM, God Himself, to which the entire cohort of soldiers fell to the ground. Now they really thought that they could bind Him? Did they use rope? Or chains?

Here is a word to the wise.

No human rope or man-made chain could ever hold our Savior. Jesus was constrained solely by the chains of divine love for us. Praise God!

Today I will apply this wisdom in my life in the following ways:

_____

_____

To listen to this
Word to the Wise,
use your smart device
to scan the QR code!

October 20

Vanity, Vanity; All is Vanity

Ecclesiastes 12

What is the core of your unhappiness?

I suspect that much of our unhappiness is generated from our attachments to what is external and temporal and not that which is honoring to God. We build our lives on objects, activities, and even people.

Here's a question – what are you building your life on? Here is a word to the wise.

When we are preoccupied with this quest for happiness and those things that God created and not God Himself, we are losing ourselves to that which is vanity. But according to Solomon who had everything, all is vanity. Therefore, focus on what matters most to God in your daily living. Live for Him, and your happiness will be exchanged for lasting joy.

Today I will apply this wisdom in my life in the following ways:

_____

_____

To listen to this
Word to the Wise,
use your smart device
to scan the QR code!

What Are You Known For?

Colossians 1:4-5

When others think about you, what do they really remember?

Paul said to the believers in Colossians 1:4, "We heard of your faith in Christ Jesus and the love you have for all the saints because of the hope laid up for you in heaven."

Here's a question – what are you known for? Notice the apostle Paul didn't say, "We've heard of your great *golf game* or your *ability to tell a good joke.*"

Here is a word to the wise.

Ask God to empower you to live in such a way that your faith, love, and hope are evident to all. Now, that's something others will remember long after you're gone!

Today I will apply this wisdom in my life in the following ways:

_____

_____

To listen to this
Word to the Wise,
use your smart device
to scan the QR code!

October 22

Fearless!

I Samuel 17

In life, perspective is important.

Many of us are familiar with the story of David and Goliath. Saul, the king of Israel, was afraid to fight Goliath, but David, a little shepherd boy, fought him and won.

Here's a question – what did David have that Saul didn't? Saul saw Goliath from man's perspective and was afraid. David saw Goliath from God's perspective and was fearless.

So, what's the difference? Here is a word to the wise.

When facing your giants, what is your perspective? We can face life with confidence if we remember, like David, the battle is not ours, but the Lord's!

Today I will apply this wisdom in my life in the following ways:

_____

_____

To listen to this
Word to the Wise,
use your smart device
to scan the QR code!

October 23

Name Game

I John 3:4

Recently someone gave me this interesting article, "What is sin? Man calls sin an accident; God calls it an abomination. Man calls it liberty; God calls it lawlessness. Man calls it a mistake; God calls it madness. Man calls it a weakness; but God calls it willfulness."

If you're giving warm and fuzzy names to your sin, here is a word to the wise.

First John 3:4 says, "Everyone who practices sin also practices lawlessness, and sin is lawlessness." The Bible calls it sin. Ask God to help you deal with the real issue — repentance.

Today I will apply this wisdom in my life in the following ways:

_____

_____

To listen to this
Word to the Wise,
use your smart device
to scan the QR code!

October 24

Ultimate in Joy

Do you hunger for fulfillment, meaning, and purpose?

One of the most powerful obstacles that keep us from making our lives count for something great is diversion.

Here is a word to the wise.

When we find our resources, time, and energy being absorbed by trivial and unimportant matters, we ultimately give God our leftovers. As a result, our ability to love others becomes anemic, marginal, and uneventful.

But if you would follow the two greatest commandments in Scripture, namely, loving God and loving others, then you will discover that it is **in God** where ultimate joy, meaning, and significance are found.

Today I will apply this wisdom in my life in the following ways:

_____

_____

To listen to this
Word to the Wise,
use your smart device
to scan the QR code!

October 25

If He Holds the Universe

Genesis 18:14

Ninety-three million miles – that's the distance between our planet and the sun.

It's the perfect distance to sustain life, provide heat and energy, and stay in the orbit.

Here is a word to the wise.

If God can hold every star in place, think of how capable He is at handling your toughest problem. The question is asked in Genesis 18:14, "Is anything too difficult for the Lord?" Our entire universe rests carefully on many delicate balances, and we don't worry about any of it.

So, stop worrying about your smaller problems and cast your cares on Him – for He cares for **you**.

Today I will apply this wisdom in my life in the following ways:

_____

_____

To listen to this
Word to the Wise,
use your smart device
to scan the QR code!

October 26

What's Behind Door #1?

Genesis 25

Do you remember the game show, "Let's Make a Deal"?

During each show, Monty Hall would present the winning contestant the opportunity to trade their winnings in for a chance to win a bigger prize. The temptation is that there's a better deal behind a numbered door.

In Genesis Chapter 25, Esau's profane character led him to trade his godly inheritance in for a single meal that brought only temporary satisfaction.

Are you in a desperate situation where you're thinking about abandoning your faith for what appears to be a better way? Here is a word to the wise.

If you want to live a life without compromise, the only **door** to safety **is Jesus**.

Today I will apply this wisdom in my life in the following ways:

_____

_____

To listen to this
Word to the Wise,
use your smart device
to scan the QR code!

October 27

Don't Be Found Sleeping

Luke 22:42

When you're faced with temptations, what do you do?

In the Garden of Gethsemane just prior to His arrest, Jesus was in deep agony, but He prayed, according to Luke 22:42, saying, "Father, if You are willing, remove this cup from Me. Yet, not My will but Yours be done."

Jesus saw the sinfulness of sin in its true colors, but as painful as it was and as repugnant as it was, Jesus was obedient to the Father's will. In contrast, the disciples were asked to pray and they fell asleep.

Here is a word to the wise.

If you are faced with dangers and problems, don't fall asleep. Take it to God in prayer.

Today I will apply this wisdom in my life in the following ways:

_____

_____

To listen to this
Word to the Wise,
use your smart device
to scan the QR code!

Sin of Selfishness

James 1:27

Paul David Tripp said, "Sin will make you think that you're the most important person in the universe."

Did you know that the sin of selfishness will impact your willingness to serve others? James 1:27 says, "Pure and undefiled religion in the sight of our God and Father is this, to visit orphans and widows in their distress."

Are you the center of God's ministry? Here is a word to the wise.

In order to adequately serve the needy, we must first deny ourselves, pick up our cross daily, and follow Jesus. When we do this, we'll cleanse ourselves from the influence of the world, which encourages us to pursue selfishness.

Today I will apply this wisdom in my life in the following ways:

_____

_____

To listen to this
Word to the Wise,
use your smart device
to scan the QR code!

302

October 29

What Do You Lack?

I Samuel 31

One of my favorite Haddon Robinson stories is about a guy named Steve Lach, a football player from the University of North Carolina. He was so good they made a cheer about him. "Steve Lach, Steve Lach, what does he lack? *Nothing! Nothing! Nothing!*"

Steve graduated and dropped into obscurity until a notice in the paper said he was returning to school, but this time working in the equipment room. He just had been released from a state institution while beginning his road back to fame.

Are you lacking in anything? Here is a word to the wise.

In I Samuel 31, Saul started out well but ended spiritually bankrupt. While King Saul had everything, he was lacking one thing – faith in God. Without faith in God, we have *nothing, nothing, nothing.*

Today I will apply this wisdom in my life in the following ways:

_____

_____

To listen to this *Word to the Wise,* use your smart device to scan the QR code!

October 30

What Impresses You?

Mark 13

In Mark 13, Jesus' disciples were marveling at the architecture of the temple, but they were dull to the spiritual realities around them.

Jesus proceeded to teach them of the things to come and called them to be on the alert.

If you find it difficult to stay spiritually alert, here is a word to the wise.

Jesus promises that He will indeed come back, though the day and hour no one knows. Keep your relationship with Him current. Talk to Him throughout your day and listen to Him through reading His Word.

As you grow in intimacy with Christ, you'll become less impressed with earthly things and more prone to marvel at His patience and grace.

Today I will apply this wisdom in my life in the following ways:

_____

_____

To listen to this
Word to the Wise,
use your smart device
to scan the QR code!

Good News of a Crushed Skull

Genesis 3:15

Did you know that the first prophecy of good news in the Scriptures included the promise of war and a crushed skull?

In Genesis 3:15, God told Satan, "There will be a war between you and the woman and between your seed and her Seed. By Him will your head be crushed." Now, how is that a prophecy of good news?

Here is a word to the wise.

God promised that the Seed of a woman would be born to defeat the one who led man into sin. In Jesus, God became man, conquered death, and offers eternal life to sinners who believe. Now, that's good news!

Today I will apply this wisdom in my life in the following ways:

_____

_____

To listen to this
Word to the Wise,
use your smart device
to scan the QR code!

November 1

Groan or Grumble?

Philippians 2:14

Charles Spurgeon has said, "God's people may groan, but they may not grumble."

The Psalms make it clear that we can cry out to God in our troubles, but Philippians 2:14 reminds us to "do everything without grumbling."

If you have a tendency to growl rather than glorify God in your troubles, here is a word to the wise.

The next time you're tempted to grumble or growl, go to Jesus and groan. He knows and He cares. Your groaning will one day give way to glory, and one millisecond in Christ's presence will far outweigh all the pain we experience here on earth.

Today I will apply this wisdom in my life in the following ways:

_____

_____

To listen to this
Word to the Wise,
use your smart device
to scan the QR code!

Biblical Clarity in an Age of Confusion

Mark 12:24

Here at the College of Biblical Studies, our fortieth anniversary celebration theme is "Biblical Clarity in an Age of Confusion."

We are absolutely convinced that the Scriptures are both clear and sufficient in addressing all the issues that pertain to living a godly life.

Our world is in confusion because, as Jesus said in Mark 12:24, people "don't understand the Scriptures or the power of God."

If you sense a growing fog of confusion descending in our society, here is a word to the wise.

Make an intentional effort to study God's Word. Our *Bible Study Methods* course will dissipate the fog and equip you to let **your** light shine for Christ.

Today I will apply this wisdom in my life in the following ways:

_____

_____

To listen to this
Word to the Wise,
use your smart device
to scan the QR code!

November 3

Climate of Compassion

Titus 3:2

Have you ever noticed a sense of anger and outrage when it comes to politics?

God calls believers in Titus 3:2 to "malign no one, to be peaceable and gentle," for we also once were foolish ourselves, but in God's grace, Jesus Christ saved us.

If you're feeling the mounting frustration of all the political foolishness going around in this world, here is a word to the wise.

Remember the kindness of God in Christ and His love for mankind. Let the foolishness of this world compel you to tell others about Jesus, and how He saved you from a life of anger and delivered you to a life of love.

Today I will apply this wisdom in my life in the following ways:

_____

_____

To listen to this
Word to the Wise,
use your smart device
to scan the QR code!

November 4

What's Your Citizen Status?

Philippians 1:27

Andrew Jackson said, "Every good citizen makes his country's honor his own."

Speaking to believers in Philippians 1:27, the apostle Paul wrote, "Above all, you must live as citizens of heaven, conducting yourselves in a manner worthy of the good news about Christ."

If politics seem to be more relevant than proclaiming Christ, here is a word to the wise.

As important as it is to be a good citizen in our great country, it is infinitely more important that we live as citizens of heaven. So, go ahead, stay current on the latest political news, but let your life and your lips represent Jesus Christ as King.

Today I will apply this wisdom in my life in the following ways:

_____

_____

To listen to this
Word to the Wise,
use your smart device
to scan the QR code!

November 5

Pontificating on Politics

I Timothy 2:1-2

What should be a Christian's preeminent role in politics?

First Timothy 2:1-2 says, "First of all then, I urge that prayers be made on behalf of all men, for kings, and all who are in authority."

If you've never considered prayer as a means of political activism, here is a word to the wise.

Speaking evil of leaders is not the path of godliness, dignity, or peace. As believers, our first priority in politics is to pray for the salvation of our political leaders. Before we pontificate on politics, let us make sure we are genuinely praying for our politicians.

Today I will apply this wisdom in my life in the following ways:

_____

_____

To listen to this
Word to the Wise,
use your smart device
to scan the QR code!

November 6

Value of Truth

Proverbs 23:23

What is the most valuable purchase that you'll ever make? A business? A home?

Proverbs 23:23 says, "Buy truth and do not sell it. Get wisdom and instruction and understanding."

If you've never thought of truth as something that comes with a price, here is a word to the wise.

Truth comes at a cost of forsaking wrong thinking. Wisdom comes at the expense of forsaking foolishness. So buy truth and never sell it. Truth is priceless. Why? Because the truth of Jesus sets us free.

Today I will apply this wisdom in my life in the following ways:

_____

_____

To listen to this
Word to the Wise,
use your smart device
to scan the QR code!

November 7

A Sure Bet

Proverbs 3:5-6; 16:33

You've probably heard it said, "I'd rather be lucky than good." Proverbs 16:33 says, "The lot is cast into the lap, but its every decision is from the LORD." Nothing is outside of His sovereign care. So, how do you respond to life when you feel down and out?

Here is a word to the wise.

Proverbs 3 says, "Trust in the Lord with all your heart and don't lean on your own understanding. In all of your ways acknowledge Him, and He will direct your path." Stop gambling on your own solution. Obey Christ. He is the only sure bet!

Today I will apply this wisdom in my life in the following ways:

_____

_____

To listen to this
Word to the Wise,
use your smart device
to scan the QR code!

He Will Provide!

Genesis 22:8

It's been said, "Provision is God's responsibility, not ours. We are merely called to commit what we have."

In Genesis 22, God called Abraham to offer his son as a burnt offering. That day, God provided a ram as a substitute for Isaac.

If you've ever struggled with a troublesome test of faith, here is a word to the wise.

Difficult tests refine and strengthen our faith which leads to greater hope and endurance. No matter the test, commit all that you have, and trust in God. He will provide!

Today I will apply this wisdom in my life in the following ways:

_____

_____

To listen to this
Word to the Wise,
use your smart device
to scan the QR code!

November 9

Treasure vs. Tension

Proverbs 21:20

According to one poll, one-third of those who make $75,000 annually live paycheck-to-paycheck.

Proverbs 21:20 says, "There is precious treasure and oil in the dwelling of the wise, but a foolish man swallows it up."

If you're wondering how to accumulate some of that precious treasure instead of precarious feelings of tension, here is a word to the wise.

Whether you make $10 an hour or $75,000 a year, don't devour everything you make. Put some aside for a rainy day. Purpose to spend less than you make. Over time you'll find your treasure growing and your tension shrinking.

Today I will apply this wisdom in my life in the following ways:

_____

_____

To listen to this
Word to the Wise,
use your smart device
to scan the QR code!

November 10

Stay Tuned for Further Alerts

Proverbs 15:10

Do you get angry when you hear the obnoxious beeping of the Emergency Broadcast System on your radio or TV, and turn it off?

Or do you continue to listen so that you are informed of any imminent danger?

Then why do we so often turn away from those who warn us of spiritual dangers we may be facing?

Here is a word to the wise.

Proverbs 15:10 says, "Whoever abandons the right path will be severely disciplined. Whoever hates correction will die." As hard as it is, don't recoil at criticism. Listen to the warning and then take the appropriate action. If the danger doesn't apply to you, go back to the pleasant music. If it does, stay tuned for *further* alerts.

Today I will apply this wisdom in my life in the following ways:

_____

_____

To listen to this
Word to the Wise,
use your smart device
to scan the QR code!

November 11

Press on Through the Darkness

John 1:5

Tolkien said, "Faithless is he that says farewell when the road darkens."

John 1:5 tells us, "The light shines in the darkness and the darkness can never extinguish it."

If you've ever been tempted to say farewell to the life of faith because the road seems so poorly lit and desolate, here is a word to the wise.

No matter how dark the road may look in this world, those who have faith in Christ must press on and look to the true light glimmering in the distance. Keep following the light in the darkness, because God has promised that it leads to an eternity where there will be no darkness at all.

Today I will apply this wisdom in my life in the following ways:

_____

_____

To listen to this
Word to the Wise,
use your smart device
to scan the QR code!

Night Light

John 8:12

Have you ever gotten up in the middle of the night and stubbed your toe in the dark? The Bible declares that the whole world is in spiritual darkness and much more is at stake than a sore toe!

Jesus said in John 8:12, "I am the light of the world. He who follows Me will not walk in darkness but will have the light of life."

If you see others limping around spiritually, looking for that light switch, here is a word to the wise.

Lend a hand to those who are stumbling in pain and groping in the night. If Jesus lives in you, you are the lamp that can lead them out of darkness. Tell them about Christ and that faith in Him is the switch that will turn their darkness into light!

Today I will apply this wisdom in my life in the following ways:

_____

_____

To listen to this
Word to the Wise,
use your smart device
to scan the QR code!

November 13

Easy for Us to Say

Mark 2:5

Which is harder to say? Your sins are forgiven, or to tell a lame man that he is healed and he can get up and walk? That's the question Jesus asked in Mark 2.

Actually, it must have been extremely difficult for Jesus to say, "Your sins are forgiven" – much more difficult than "pick up your pallet and walk."

Why? Here is a word to the wise.

Jesus knew what it would cost – the price He Himself would pay to forgive our sins. He would endure the righteous wrath of God. Forgiveness may be easy for us to say, but remember how difficult it was for Jesus to purchase. Praise God that He declared, "Your sins *are* forgiven."

Today I will apply this wisdom in my life in the following ways:

_____

_____

To listen to this
Word to the Wise,
use your smart device
to scan the QR code!

318

Ability vs. Privilege

Proverbs 17:2

Have you ever wished you had been born into a rich and influential family?

Imagine the things you could achieve with just a little better start in life. Proverbs 17:2 says, however, "A servant who acts wisely will rule over a son who acts shamefully and will share in the inheritance among brothers."

If you think you are behind in life, here is a word to the wise.

Never underestimate the abilities God has given you. Give yourself and your abilities completely over to Christ and you will see where He takes you. In the end, being born in His family is all the privilege you will ever need.

Today I will apply this wisdom in my life in the following ways:

_____

_____

To listen to this
Word to the Wise,
use your smart device
to scan the QR code!

Self-Inflicted Tongue Lashing

Proverbs 14:3; Colossians 4:6

Do you take pride in "telling it like it is"?

Proverbs 14:3 reads, "In the mouth of the foolish is a rod for his back, but the lips of the wise will protect them."

If your words have ever been a rod for your back, here is a word to the wise.

God does call believers to speak the truth in love. However, He also says, "Let your speech be seasoned with grace." We need to know when and how to speak as Christians.

Pray for God's wisdom and pay close attention to His Word. If you do, you'll find safety in your speech rather than a lashing caused by your own lips.

Today I will apply this wisdom in my life in the following ways:

_____

_____

To listen to this
Word to the Wise,
use your smart device
to scan the QR code!

November 16

The Promise and the Process

Genesis 21:5

One writer said, "Waiting is not just something we have to do until we get what we want. Waiting is part of the process of becoming what God wants us to be."

In Genesis 21, a quarter of a century after He had promised that Abraham would become a great nation, God gave him his first legitimate heir, and Abraham was a hundred years old!

If you feel that you've been waiting on God's promised blessings a long time, here is a word to the wise.

God is doing something *in* your waiting. He is revealing your weaknesses, developing your character, and ultimately strengthening your faith. Remember, it's not only the **promise** that matters, but also the **process**.

Today I will apply this wisdom in my life in the following ways:

_____

_____

To listen to this
Word to the Wise,
use your smart device
to scan the QR code!

November 17

Keep Looking to Your Reward

Hebrews 11:24-26

George Müller said, "Wherever God has given faith, it is given for the very purpose of being tried."

Faith will always be tested so that it reveals what one really believes.

Hebrews 11:24 tells us, "By faith Moses refused to be called the son of Pharaoh's daughter, choosing rather the reproach of Christ over all the riches of Egypt." Moses chose suffering for Christ over being set for life. Why?

Here is a word to the wise.

He was looking for his eternal reward. If God has given you faith, it will be tried. But keep looking to your reward – **eternity with Christ**.

Today I will apply this wisdom in my life in the following ways:

_____

_____

To listen to this
Word to the Wise,
use your smart device
to scan the QR code!

Is It from God?

James 3:13-18

With all the self-help books, blogs, and other sources of information in the world today, how can we identify godly wisdom?

James 3 tells us that worldly wisdom involves envy and selfish ambition. But the wisdom from above is first pure, then peaceable, gentle, reasonable, full of mercy, and without hypocrisy.

If you are having trouble distinguishing godly wisdom from worldly wisdom, here is a word to the wise.

The next time you're offered advice, test it! Does this involve humility and holiness, or selfish ambition? You'll never go wrong when you attend to the things that make for peace, act in mercy, and avoid hypocrisy.

Today I will apply this wisdom in my life in the following ways:

_____

_____

To listen to this
Word to the Wise,
use your smart device
to scan the QR code!

November 19

Interceding for Others

Genesis 18:22-33

Someone has said, "We are never more like Christ than in prayers of intercession."

In Genesis 18, Abraham asked God to spare all in Sodom if he could find ten believers. Sadly, there weren't even ten. In mercy, however, God spared Lot and his daughters.

If you're praying for friends or family living too close to the world, here is a word to the wise.

Sometimes God calls us to intercede for others when they themselves are too weak spiritually to see the danger. Never stop praying for those who are struggling! God may use your intercession to deliver those headed for destruction.

Today I will apply this wisdom in my life in the following ways:

_____

_____

To listen to this
Word to the Wise,
use your smart device
to scan the QR code!

November 20

The Smile That Really Matters

Proverbs 11:12

Everyone enjoys making other people smile, but how often do we smile or make others smile by making light of someone else?

Proverbs 11:12 says, "It is foolish to belittle one's neighbor. A sensible person keeps quiet."

If you've ever made someone else the butt of your joke, here is a word to the wise.

Sarcastic jokes and put-downs may seem funny for a moment, but they rarely have anything to do with love. Ask God to grant you words that build others up as you seek to honor Him and others with your lips. You'll discern the smile of God, *and that's the smile that really matters.*

Today I will apply this wisdom in my life in the following ways:

_____

_____

To listen to this
Word to the Wise,
use your smart device
to scan the QR code!

November 21

Pursuit of Holiness

Hebrews 12:14

Someone said, "If the doctrine of sinless perfection is a heresy, the doctrine of contentment with sinful imperfection is a greater heresy."

Just because you'll never be sinless in this life is no reason to give up fighting sin. God's Word commands us to continue the fight. Hebrews 12:14 says, "Pursue holiness, for without it no one will see the Lord."

If you've noticed a lull in your passion to pursue holiness, here is a word to the wise.

Embrace the pursuit of holiness. God's Spirit will strengthen you for the fight, and God's grace will encourage you in the battle.

Today I will apply this wisdom in my life in the following ways:

_____

_____

To listen to this
Word to the Wise,
use your smart device
to scan the QR code!

Paradise on Earth?

Genesis 13:10

Irwin Lutzer said, "Few people have the spiritual resources to be both wealthy and godly."

Both Abraham and Lot were rich, but only Abraham evidenced a wealth of spiritual resources. Genesis 13 says that Lot chose to live in the land that seemed to be like paradise, even though the men of the place were wicked.

If you struggle with wanting greener pastures, here is a word to the wise.

You know how Lot's story ended. He was constantly tempted to compromise and eventually lost all of his earthly possessions.

Don't impoverish yourself spiritually with a false promise of paradise on earth. Eternal riches await those who wait on the Lord.

Today I will apply this wisdom in my life in the following ways:

_____

_____

To listen to this
Word to the Wise,
use your smart device
to scan the QR code!

Foolish Thinking

Genesis 16

Have you ever tried to accomplish God's will by relying on your own wisdom rather than His?

In Genesis 16, Abraham decided to pursue God's promise by listening to Sarah's advice and taking her handmaid as a secondary wife. A son was indeed born, but not the son God promised. In fact, the son became a rival to the promised heir, Isaac.

If you are tempted to believe that the end justifies the means, here is a word to the wise.

Do not be fooled. Worldly wisdom causes you to compromise God's standards. Don't trust your own wisdom. Look to the Lord! He is always faithful to do what He has promised.

Today I will apply this wisdom in my life in the following ways:

_____

_____

To listen to this
Word to the Wise,
use your smart device
to scan the QR code!

Day of Reckoning

Ecclesiastes 12:13-14

Ecclesiastes tells us that without the right view of eternity, there is very little difference between a wise man and a fool, because death is the end of both.

How important is it to believe in the Bible's testimony of the future day of reckoning for all men? Here is a word to the wise.

Solomon wanted us to see the futility of life lived apart from the biblical view of eternity. He concludes in Ecclesiastes 12, "Fear God and keep His commandments, for God will bring every act to judgment and everything which is hidden." Everything!

So trust Jesus. He is the Savior who will deliver on the day of reckoning.

Today I will apply this wisdom in my life in the following ways:

_____

_____

To listen to this
Word to the Wise,
use your smart device
to scan the QR code!

November 25

On-the-Job Training

Genesis 6:22

How would you feel if God told you to build a giant cruise ship, *and your life depended on it?* Can you imagine how Noah must have felt?

But in Genesis 6, it says that Noah found grace in the eyes of the Lord and, "Thus, Noah did; according to all that God had commanded him."

If you are feeling overwhelmed by what God is calling you to do, here is a word to the wise.

Noah had to start from somewhere and learn on the job. Learn to obey God's Word step-by-step, day-by-day, and as you walk with God in obedience to His Word – because of His grace – even you can do the incredible!

Today I will apply this wisdom in my life in the following ways:

_____

_____

To listen to this
Word to the Wise,
use your smart device
to scan the QR code!

November 26

From Fertilizer to Flowers

Psalm 119:67

An old Puritan pastor wrote, "The snow covers many a dunghill; so does prosperity many a rotten heart."

When life seems easy, we often don't see what's really in our heart. Psalm 119:67 says, "Before I was afflicted I went astray, but now I keep Your Word."

If you've ever seen the lovely veneer of your life melt into a manure pile, here is a word to the wise.

Let affliction compel you to seek the Lord. Receive His grace and submit to His Word. When you do, you'll see the fertilizer yield glorious flowers of joy and lasting contentment.

Today I will apply this wisdom in my life in the following ways:

_____

_____

To listen to this
Word to the Wise,
use your smart device
to scan the QR code!

November 27

Let's Make a Deal

Proverbs 20:25

Have you ever played *Let's Make a Deal* with God?

"Lord, if You do this for me, I'll do this or that." Most of us have at least thought about such divine *bargaining*.

Proverbs 20:25 says, "Don't trap yourself by making a rash promise to God, only later counting the cost."

If you have ever played that game with God, here is a word to the wise.

Our Father is infinitely holy and not to be trifled with, but He is also unbelievably gracious and full of compassion. Don't play games with God. Ask Jesus for help, and you'll be surprised that the only thing you need is divine *mercy*.

Today I will apply this wisdom in my life in the following ways:

_____

_____

To listen to this
Word to the Wise,
use your smart device
to scan the QR code!

November 28

Kill or Be Killed

Genesis 4:7

It's been said, "Sin has dug every grave."

In Genesis 4, Cain was unhappy that God did not accept his offering. The Lord warned Cain by saying, "Sin is crouching at the door and its desire is for you, but you must master it." Cain became bitter and sin led him to murder his brother.

How do you respond when God's Word convicts you of sin? Here is a word to the wise.

While sin may not lead us to actual homicide, make no mistake, it's just as deadly. Don't wait! Call on God for the grace-empowered strength to kill that sin **before it kills you**.

Today I will apply this wisdom in my life in the following ways:

_____

_____

To listen to this
Word to the Wise,
use your smart device
to scan the QR code!

November 29

Why Do We Pray?

Genesis 25:21

If God is sovereign, why should we pray?

Genesis tells us that before Isaac was even born, God promised a great nation would come through him. Yet for the first twenty years of his marriage, he was childless. But Genesis 25:21 says, "Isaac prayed to the LORD on behalf of his wife, because she was barren; and the LORD answered him and Rebekah his wife conceived."

If you've ever doubted the necessity of prayer in God's plan, here is a word to the wise.

God commands prayer as the avenue by which He accomplishes His sovereign purposes. Pray with great anticipation, because it is the means by which His kingdom comes and His will is done!

Today I will apply this wisdom in my life in the following ways:

_____

_____

To listen to this
Word to the Wise,
use your smart device
to scan the QR code!

November 30

Don't Tap Out!

Ephesians 4:31

How would you describe your family gathering? A walk in the park? A day at the zoo? Or a WWE wrestling match?

Ephesians 4:31 provides a great guide for families. It says, "Let all bitterness and wrath and anger and clamor and slander be put away from you, along with all malice. Be kind to one another, tenderhearted, forgiving each other just as God in Christ also has forgiven you."

So how do you get your family to look like the gospel? Here is a word to the wise.

Let all bitterness and anger go, stop the slander and malice, be kind, forgive, <u>and stay out of the ring!</u>

Today I will apply this wisdom in my life in the following ways:

_____

_____

To listen to this
Word to the Wise,
use your smart device
to scan the QR code!

December 1

Ultimate Fulfillment

II Peter 1:3

Lewis Sperry Chafer once said, "The Bible is not such a book a man would write if he could or could write if he would."

Here at the College of Biblical Studies, we are convinced that the Bible is God's Word and sufficient to fully equip us spiritually. As II Peter 1:3 highlights, we have everything that pertains to life and godliness through the true knowledge of Christ.

If you're feeling like something is missing from your life, here is a word to the wise.

There may be a place for self-help books and seminars, but growing in the true knowledge of Christ is the missing link to finding ultimate fulfillment.

Today I will apply this wisdom in my life in the following ways:

_____

_____

To listen to this
Word to the Wise,
use your smart device
to scan the QR code!

December 2

You're in Good Hands

Psalm 147:5

One of the more popular car insurance slogans says, "You're in good hands with Allstate."

However, if we are not in the driver's seat, sometimes we can become fearful and doubtful because our lives are in someone else's hands.

Do you trust God in the driver's seat? If not, here is a word to the wise.

Psalm 147:5 says, "Great is our Lord and mighty in power. His understanding has no limit." Believe it or not, God knows more about what is best for us than we do. Let Him take control of your life, and try not to be a backseat driver.

Truly, with God, you're in good hands!

Today I will apply this wisdom in my life in the following ways:

To listen to this
Word to the Wise,
use your smart device
to scan the QR code!

Tie Your Shoes!

Ephesians 6:15

Have you ever slipped and fallen flat on your backside? It's not only embarrassing; it can hurt.

Unfortunately, in our world today many believers are spiritually falling and not only hurting themselves but their families and friends as well. In Ephesians 6, Paul calls believers to stand firm by having shoes that are prepared by the gospel of peace. Believers have the good news of Christ's salvation to always guarantee their peace with God.

If you are feeling yourself losing traction in the spiritual battle, here is a word to the wise.

Remember who Christ is and that He has secured your peace. Tie your shoes and stand firm in the faith!

Today I will apply this wisdom in my life in the following ways:

_____

_____

To listen to this
Word to the Wise,
use your smart device
to scan the QR code!

December 4

Get Back in the (Prayer) Closet!

Mark 1:35

How is your prayer life?

Did you know that prayer for a Christian should not only be a necessity, but also a way of life?

Mark 1:35 says, "In the early morning while it was still dark, Jesus got up, left the house, and went away to a secluded place and was praying there."

If you want to improve your prayer life, here is a word to the wise.

Make prayer a priority. Set a consistent time. Find a quiet place where you can spend some quality time with God.

Otis Hawkins once said, "If He who never sinned saw the need of private prayer alone with the Father, how much more do we?"

Today I will apply this wisdom in my life in the following ways:

_____

_____

To listen to this *Word to the Wise,* use your smart device to scan the QR code!

December 5

I Don't Get It

Luke 18:34

Do you ever wonder why some people just don't get it?

In Luke 18, we're told that Jesus clearly explained to His disciples that He would be betrayed, killed, and then rise from the dead. But it says in verse 34, "They didn't understand any of this."

If it is hard to understand why *they* didn't understand, here is a word to the wise.

Like the disciples, sometimes we don't comprehend the simple truth revealed in God's Word. Ask the Lord to help you *get* the things you should, and thank Him for His incredible patience and grace when you don't.

Today I will apply this wisdom in my life in the following ways:

_____

_____

To listen to this
Word to the Wise,
use your smart device
to scan the QR code!

December 6

Crown Wearers and Cross Bearers

I Peter 2:21-23

Charles Spurgeon said, "There are no crown wearers in heaven who are not cross bearers here below."

As a Christian, do you often get tired of bearing your cross? Do you at times desire to retaliate against those who have wronged you?

Before you lose your control, here is a word to the wise.

Peter tells us how Jesus responded in I Peter 2:23: "He uttered no threats but kept entrusting Himself to Him who judges righteously." First, ask God to hold your peace when you feel that you are being crucified. Secondly, trust in Him who has prepared your cross uniquely for your crown.

Today I will apply this wisdom in my life in the following ways:

_____

_____

To listen to this
Word to the Wise,
use your smart device
to scan the QR code!

December 7

Spiritual Net Worth

James 1:11

Billy Graham said, "There's nothing wrong with men possessing riches. The wrong comes when riches possess men."

James 1:11 speaks of the folly of boasting in riches. Like the grass that withers in the heat of the sun, the rich man will wither away while pursuing his activities.

If you have wrestled with how to view your financial state, here is a word to the wise.

Wealth is not always an indicator of God's favor, and poverty is not always an indicator of a divine frown. Whatever your net worth is in this life, the riches of Christ are what bring lasting delight.

Today I will apply this wisdom in my life in the following ways:

_____

_____

To listen to this
Word to the Wise,
use your smart device
to scan the QR code!

December 8

Percentages and the Christian Walk

Ephesians 2:10

Augustine said, "Without God, we cannot. Without us, He will not."

Do you struggle with a relationship between divine sovereignty and human responsibility? Ephesians 2:10 says, "For we are His workmanship, created in Christ Jesus for good works which God prepared beforehand so that we would walk in them."

Here is a word to the wise.

The Bible affirms that God is one hundred percent sovereign and man is one hundred percent responsible. Ephesians 2:10 confirms that God prepared good works for us. So what are you waiting for? Get up and start walking!

Today I will apply this wisdom in my life in the following ways:

_____

_____

To listen to this
Word to the Wise,
use your smart device
to scan the QR code!

December 9

Blind Faith

Genesis 12:1-4

It's been said, "The evidence of knowing God is obeying God."

In Genesis 12, God called Abraham to leave all that he knew to go to a land that He would show him. The Lord promised blessing, but Abraham had no tangible proof, only a promise.

If you're looking for proof of His blessing before you obey, here is a word to the wise.

Abraham went forth as the Lord had spoken to him. Even though he had never seen the distant land, Abraham trusted God's word. Don't wait for evidence of blessing before you obey. Trust His promises and walk in His way!

Today I will apply this wisdom in my life in the following ways:

_____

_____

To listen to this
Word to the Wise,
use your smart device
to scan the QR code!

December 10

Lunar Landing vs. Love

I Corinthians 13:4

Ralph Cramden on "The Honeymooners" would always scream at his wife, Alice, for every little reason: "To the moon, Alice! To the moon!"

Ralph had very little patience in his marriage. Here's a question for you. Do you struggle with patience in your marriage? Paul says in I Corinthians 13:4, "Love is patient."

If you want to improve your relationship, here is a word to the wise.

Ask God to give you a calm spirit and to love your spouse even when they are wrong. When you do this God's way through love, He won't take your spouse to the moon, but He **will** give you a marriage that's on track for "heaven!"

Today I will apply this wisdom in my life in the following ways:

_____

_____

To listen to this
Word to the Wise,
use your smart device
to scan the QR code!

December 11

Are You Pouting?

James 1:2

When you hear the words "pure joy," what do you think of? Do trouble and difficulty come to mind? I don't think so.

The Bible says in James 1:2, "Consider it pure joy, my brothers, whenever you face trials."

If you struggle with joy in the midst of trials, here is a word to the wise.

God is concerned more with your character than your comfort. He says the testing of your faith produces endurance and endurance brings you to maturity in Christ. So when trouble comes, don't pout over your problems! Praise God for His promise to perfect you *through* them.

Today I will apply this wisdom in my life in the following ways:

_____

_____

To listen to this
Word to the Wise,
use your smart device
to scan the QR code!

Relax!

Philippians 4:6

Can't find your keys? Gas on "E"? Bills due? Kids driving you crazy? *"I'm forgetting to do something."* *"What's today again?"* Got a zillion things on your mind?

Just relax and breathe. Philippians 4:6 says, "Be anxious for nothing, but in everything by prayer and supplication with thanksgiving, let your requests be made known to God."

Here is a word to the wise.

The same God who created heaven and earth, and the same God you put your faith in with your eternal destination, is the same God who can handle **every single problem** that you have. So, trust Him. And Relax!

Today I will apply this wisdom in my life in the following ways:

_____

_____

To listen to this
Word to the Wise,
use your smart device
to scan the QR code!

December 13

Look for the Best or Find the Worst

Proverbs 11:27

When you think of those around you – your family, your coworkers, your friends, and even your enemies – what do you desire for them?

Proverbs 11:27 says, "If you search for good, you'll find favor, but if you search for evil, it will find you." The word translated "search" suggests waiting or watching, like someone "looking" for the dawn.

If perhaps you're more often looking for the worst to rise in people, here is a word to the wise.

As Derek Kidner says, "This proverb teaches that what you seek for others, you will get yourself." Always look for the best in and for others. If you don't, you will eventually discover the worst in yourself.

Today I will apply this wisdom in my life in the following ways:

_____

_____

To listen to this
Word to the Wise,
use your smart device
to scan the QR code!

December 14

Misplaced Priorities

I Thessalonians 3:10

As a Christian, we know our primary focus should be on serving God by loving people and not things.

Yet, for many of us, it's easy to let things crowd out the people. Paul's priorities were always focused on people. He poured his life out by equipping people with the gospel. In I Thessalonians 3:10, it says, "Night and day we pray most earnestly that we may see you again and supply what is lacking in your faith."

If you're struggling with your biblical priorities, here is a word to the wise.

Prayerfully ask God to illuminate any misplaced priorities and your desire to focus on those whom God has entrusted to you.

Today I will apply this wisdom in my life in the following ways:

_____

_____

To listen to this
Word to the Wise,
use your smart device
to scan the QR code!

December 15

I Shall Not Want?

Psalm 23

What do you want in life?

The word "want" in our day means wish or desire. In days past, the English word "want" meant to lack a necessity. So, what do you really lack in life? Food? Shelter? Respect? Love?

Here is a word to the wise.

Psalm 23 says, "The Lord is my shepherd. I shall not want." If the Lord is your protector, provider, guide, and your owner you don't need anything else. He will lead you in the right way. He ensures your victory in the end. Goodness and love will ever follow you and you will dwell in His presence forever. Think about it. What do you really **_want_** in life?

Today I will apply this wisdom in my life in the following ways:

To listen to this
Word to the Wise,
use your smart device
to scan the QR code!

December 16

Thank You, Jesus!

Ephesians 2:8-9

Long after the excitement has died down, I like to raise the question to children, "Do you remember what you received as a gift for Christmas?" After a few moments of silence and a very puzzled look, the answer is normally, "No," or, "Yes, but it's broken."

Just like children, we don't remember the important value of gifts. As Christians, we sometimes forget that the most important gift from God is not earned by merit. According to Ephesians 2:8-9, Paul says, "For by grace you have been saved through faith, and it's not of your own doing. It is a gift from God."

Here is a word to the wise.

Remember to give thanks to God today for salvation and grace.

Today I will apply this wisdom in my life in the following ways:

_____

_____

To listen to this
Word to the Wise,
use your smart device
to scan the QR code!

December 17

What's in a Name?

Genesis 10

When was the last time you read a genealogical list of names you've never heard of? Did you find it interesting?

Genesis 10 and 11 record two branches of a family tree descending from Shem, the son of Noah — and they are of life and death in importance. Why? Because nothing in the Bible is without purpose.

Here is a word to the wise.

Luke 3 records the genealogy of Jesus Christ — and you guessed it, He is a descendant of Shem. So, the next time you are tempted to pass over a section of Scripture, remember the lesson of Shem's family tree. You may not always get it, but God does not waste His words.

Today I will apply this wisdom in my life in the following ways:

_____

_____

To listen to this
Word to the Wise,
use your smart device
to scan the QR code!

December 18

All He Wants for Christmas

Luke 10:41

The National Retail Federation recently announced it expects sales in November and December to hit a whopping $616.9 billion.

That's a lot of stuff. In our market-driven society, it is easy to succumb to busyness and reckless spending.

If you're tired of running and spending this holiday season, here is a word to the wise.

In Luke 10:41, Jesus tells a worried and troubled Martha only one thing is really necessary. During this time of year, be sure to offer Christ your personal devotion: for **it** is enough.

Today I will apply this wisdom in my life in the following ways:

_____

_____

To listen to this
Word to the Wise,
use your smart device
to scan the QR code!

December 19

Gift of Christ

Have you heard the saying, "It is better to give than to receive"?

While Christmas is about giving, the truth is that most of us expect to receive something for ourselves. While receiving gifts is not a bad thing, we should not be disappointed if we don't get what we want.

If you've been disappointed with your gifts of Christmases past, here is a word to the wise.

James D. Maxon says, "If you measure your life by what you own, the cavern of your heart will never be filled." Thank God for the *gift of Christ*. He alone can satisfy the desires of your heart.

Today I will apply this wisdom in my life in the following ways:

_____

_____

To listen to this
Word to the Wise,
use your smart device
to scan the QR code!

December 20

Let It Go

While many people will celebrate Christmas with family and friends, many more will not.

Why? Because of some misunderstanding that probably happened so long ago they can't even remember. Are you still holding on to the grudge that is prohibiting you from truly enjoying Christmas? Lewis B. Smedes wrote, "When you release the wrongdoer from the wrong, you cut a malignant tumor out of your inner life."

Here is a word to the wise.

Use this Christmas celebration to rebuild broken relationships. Just as the Lord forgave you, you should do the same. So on this Christmas, make a decision to let it go!

Today I will apply this wisdom in my life in the following ways:

_____

_____

To listen to this
Word to the Wise,
use your smart device
to scan the QR code!

December 21

Gift of Time

Luke 1:28

During this Christmas season, many Christians will spend more time shopping than they will with their loved ones.

While the world has commercialized Christmas, we as Christians should never forget the importance of the season. Gifts are good, but they are no substitute for your time.

If you're guilty of exchanging your time for gifts, here is a word to the wise.

In Luke 1:28, the angel Gabriel tells a fearful and lonely Mary, "Greetings, oh favored one, the Lord *is with you.*" Rather than getting preoccupied with purchasing lots of things, give someone a priceless gift this season – the gift of time.

Today I will apply this wisdom in my life in the following ways:

_____

_____

To listen to this
Word to the Wise,
use your smart device
to scan the QR code!

December 22

Message of Jesus

Luke 1

The carol, "Hark, the Herald Angels Sing," was written in 1739 by Charles Wesley, the brother of the famous John Wesley.

Although the title of the carol focuses on angels, the verses expound on the role of Jesus Christ as Savior. The last line explains His purpose: "Mild He lays His glory by, born that man no more may die, born to raise the sons of earth, born to give them second birth."

As you prepare this Christmas season, here is a word to the wise.

Share the message of Jesus Christ, **the real gift of Christmas**!

Today I will apply this wisdom in my life in the following ways:

_____

_____

To listen to this
Word to the Wise,
use your smart device
to scan the QR code!

December 23

Where Will You Live?

Luke 2:7

Have you ever wondered if Almighty God could relate to you?

Luke 2:7 says that Mary gave birth to Jesus, wrapped Him in swaddling cloths, and laid Him in a manger – a feeding trough which is usually found near or in some sort of shelter for beasts of burden. God humbled Himself to be born in a barn so that He could one day redeem those born in sin.

Still wondering if God can relate to you? Here is a word to the wise.

Jesus knows what it's like to live in *your world*. The question is, will you humble yourself before Him in faith so that you will live forever with Him in *His world*?

Today I will apply this wisdom in my life in the following ways:

_____

_____

To listen to this
Word to the Wise,
use your smart device
to scan the QR code!

December 24

While Shepherds Watch Their Flock by Night

Micah 5:2-4

Other than Joseph and Mary, who were the first to know that Christ was born?

No, I'm not talking about an ox or a donkey. Luke 2 says that an angel appeared, announcing the good news of His birth to some shepherds who were watching their flocks by night in the region near Bethlehem.

Why is that significant? Here is a word to the wise.

Micah 5 promised that a Savior would be born in Bethlehem and arise to shepherd His flock. The shepherds were shepherding their flocks, but One was now born who would arise to shepherd them. Take time to praise Jesus, the Good Shepherd, for watching over **you** by day and by night.

Today I will apply this wisdom in my life in the following ways:

_____

_____

To listen to this
Word to the Wise,
use your smart device
to scan the QR code!

December 25

Is There Room in *Your* Inn?

Luke 2:7

Was there really a no-vacancy sign on the Bethlehem Inn some two thousand years ago?

Actually, the Greek word for "inn" in Luke 2:7 refers to a guestroom. So why was there no guestroom available to Joseph and his wife in his own hometown?

Here is a word to the wise.

Some considered Jesus' conception and birth scandalous. This could explain the no-vacancy sign. But the truth is, in Jesus, God has come to dwell with man to save us from our sins. Is Jesus a scandal to you? Or have you gladly received Him as Immanuel, "God with us"?

Today I will apply this wisdom in my life in the following ways:

_____

_____

To listen to this
Word to the Wise,
use your smart device
to scan the QR code!

360

Priceless Gift of Time

Ephesians 6:4

There was this nationally renowned trial attorney who had a slogan, "A few hours with me may help you go free."

Surprisingly, his rate of $375 per hour did not stop his clients from seeking his services night and day. Since his life was so busy, his family decided to throw a late-night party for him on his birthday. As he opened his birthday cards, he discovered that his sixteen-year-old son had given him $700 in cash. He immediately said to his son, "Why?" His son replied by saying, "I wanted you to be free to spend a few hours with me."

If you are a parent, here is a word to the wise.

Make time for your children – because **they are priceless**!

Today I will apply this wisdom in my life in the following ways:

_____

_____

To listen to this
Word to the Wise,
use your smart device
to scan the QR code!

December 27

What Sets You Apart?

John 17:17

What makes a believer different from a nonbeliever? One word – truth.

In John 17:17, Jesus prayed for believers. He asked the Father to sanctify us in the truth because "God's Word is truth."

If you are struggling with the world's influence in your life, here is a word to the wise.

The truth will ultimately cause you to think and live differently from the world and grow in Christ's likeness. If you want to be more like Christ, don't simply say, "Let go and let God." Rather, let the Scriptures take hold of your heart. When you do, the Spirit of truth will set **you** apart.

Today I will apply this wisdom in my life in the following ways:

_____

_____

To listen to this
Word to the Wise,
use your smart device
to scan the QR code!

December 28

This Little Light of Mine

Philippians 2:14

Brennan Manning once said, "The greatest single cause of atheism in the world is Christians who acknowledge Jesus with their lips but deny Him with their lifestyle."

How do you live out your faith in your home, on your job, or in your community? Paul indicates in Philippians 2:14 that we should do everything without grumbling or arguing so that we may be blameless and pure children of God without blemish. Although we live in a corrupt and perverse society, we should shine as lights in the world.

Here is a word to the wise.

Living out your faith is evident in your actions toward others. Ask God to remove those tarnished spots in your behavior so that your light may shine bright.

Today I will apply this wisdom in my life in the following ways:

_____

_____

To listen to this
Word to the Wise,
use your smart device
to scan the QR code!

December 29

Mouth Muscles

James 3

Benjamin Franklin said, "Man's tongue is soft and bone doth lack; yet, a stroke therewith may break a man's back." Have you ever considered the power of your words?

James 3 says that the tongue is small, but it determines the very direction of our lives and it is harder to tame than any wild animal.

If you have trouble controlling your tongue, here is a word to the wise.

The Bible tells us that we speak out of the abundance of the heart. Fill your heart with the Scriptures and the Spirit will teach your tongue to carry a man's burden rather than break his back!

Today I will apply this wisdom in my life in the following ways:

_____

_____

To listen to this
Word to the Wise,
use your smart device
to scan the QR code!

December 30

Finish Well

II Timothy 4:5

There are some great and influential men in the Bible who started out well, but did not end as well as they could have.

King Solomon and his great grandson, King Asa, were good and godly kings overall, yet they did not finish well. It's easy for even strong believers to turn to worldly wisdom, and ever so subtly abandon their radical trust in the true and living God.

If you want to ensure you finish well, here is a word to the wise.

In II Timothy 4:5, Paul says, "Keep a clear mind in every situation." It's easy to get distracted by life's circumstances, but remember, we must keep our focus on God who keeps our minds in perfect peace.

Today I will apply this wisdom in my life in the following ways:

_____

_____

To listen to this *Word to the Wise*, use your smart device to scan the QR code!

December 31

Just Do It!

Acts 24:24-27

Do you ever think you will deal with something tomorrow when God is convicting you today?

In Acts 24, the Roman governor was frightened by Paul's teaching, but he sent him away without responding to that conviction. He would often converse with the apostle on subsequent occasions, but the Scriptures are glaringly silent about any conviction.

If God is calling you to deal with something today, here is a word to the wise.

It is very dangerous to quench the conviction of the Holy Spirit. When God is directing you, don't procrastinate. The Scripture says, "Today, if you hear His voice, do not harden your heart." What are you waiting for? **Just do it!**

Today I will apply this wisdom in my life in the following ways:

_____

_____

To listen to this
Word to the Wise,
use your smart device
to scan the QR code!